THE GREEN REV...
COOKBO...

Dave Dutton worked as a news... ... his keen sense of humour led him ... become a comedy scriptwriter, providing television material for Ken Dodd, Little and Large, Dick Emery, the two Ronnies and many other famous comedians. His other books include *The Book of Famous Oddballs* (Arrow), *Oddballs* (Arrow), *Lanky Spoken Here!* (Hobbs/Michael Joseph), *The Ken Dodd Butty Book* (Macmillan), *Ireland Strikes Back!* (Hamlyn Paperbacks) and several more.

In latter years he has taken to acting, and television roles include parts in 'Coronation Street', 'Emmerdale Farm', 'Brookside', 'Travelling Man' and several commercials. He lives in Lancashire with his wife Lynn and son Gareth and has been an enthusiastic vegetarian for many years.

He also runs 'Now You're Talking', the North's largest After Dinner Speakers' agency.

THE
GREEN
REVOLUTION
COOKBOOK

Dave Dutton

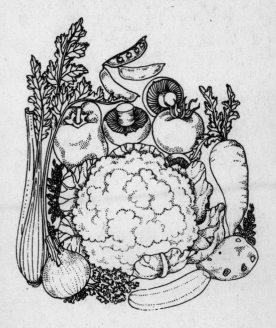

ARROW BOOKS

Arrow Books Limited
62–65 Chandos Place, London WC2N 4NW

An imprint of Century Hutchinson Limited

London Melbourne Sydney Auckland
Johannesburg and agencies throughout
the world

First published by Hamlyn Paperbacks 1981

Arrow edition 1987

© Dave Dutton 1981, 1987

Printed and bound in Great Britain by
Anchor Brendon Limited, Tiptree, Essex

ISBN 0 09 953880 6

Sir Andrew Aguecheek: I am a great eater of beef, and I
believe that does harm to my wit.
Sir Toby Belch: No question.

Twelfth Night

Contents

Useful Facts and Figures

NOTES ON METRICATION

In this book quantities are given in metric and Imperial measures. Exact conversion from Imperial to metric measures does not usually give very convenient working quantities and so the metric measures have been rounded off into units of 25 grams. The table below shows the recommended equivalents.

Ounces	Approx g to nearest whole figure	Recommended conversion to nearest unit of 25
1	28	25
2	57	50
3	85	75
4	113	100
5	142	150
6	170	175
7	198	200
8	227	225
9	255	250
10	283	275
11	312	300
12	340	350
13	368	375
14	396	400
15	425	425
16 (1lb)	454	450
17	482	475
18	510	500
19	539	550
20 (1¼lb)	567	575

Note: When converting quantities over 20 oz first add the appropriate figures in the centre column, then adjust to the nearest unit of 25. As a general guide, 1kg (1000g) equals 2.2lb or about 2lb 3 oz. This method of conversion gives good results in nearly all cases, although in certain pastry and cake recipes a more accurate conversion is necessary.

Liquid measures The millilitre has been used in this book and the following table gives a few examples.

Imperial	Approx ml to nearest whole figure	Recommended ml
¼ pint	142	150ml
½ pint	283	300ml
¾ pint	425	450ml
1 pint	567	600ml
1½ pints	851	900ml
1¾ pints	992	1000ml (1 litre)

Spoon measures All spoon measures given in this book are level unless otherwise stated.

Can sizes At present, cans are marked with the exact (usually to the nearest whole number) metric equivalent of the Imperial weight of the contents, so we have followed this practice when giving can sizes.

OVEN TEMPERATURES

The table below gives recommended equivalents.

	°C	°F	Gas Mark
Very cool	110	225	¼
	120	250	½
Cool	140	275	1
	150	300	2
Moderate	160	325	3
	180	350	4
Moderately hot	190	375	5
	200	400	6
Hot	220	425	7
	230	450	8
Very hot	240	475	9

NOTES FOR AMERICAN AND AUSTRALIAN USERS

In America the 8-oz measuring cup is used. In Australia metric measures are now used in conjunction with the standard 250-ml measuring cup. The Imperial pint, used in Britain and Australia, is 20 fl oz, while the American pint is 16 fl oz. It is important to remember that the Australian tablespoon differs from both the British and American tablespoons; the table below gives a comparison. The British standard tablespoon, which has been used throughout this book, holds 17.7 ml, the American 14.2 ml, and the Australian 20 ml. A teaspoon holds approximately 5 ml in all three countries.

British	American	Australian
1 teaspoon	1 teaspoon	1 teaspoon
1 tablespoon	1 tablespoon	1 tablespoon
2 tablespoons	3 tablespoons	2 tablespoons
3½ tablespoons	4 tablespoons	3 tablespoons
4 tablespoons	5 tablespoons	3½ tablespoons

AN IMPERIAL/AMERICAN GUIDE TO SOLID AND LIQUID MEASURES

Solid measures

IMPERIAL	AMERICAN
1 lb butter or margarine	2 cups
1 lb flour	4 cups
1 lb granulated or castor sugar	2 cups
1 lb icing sugar	3 cups
8 oz rice	1 cup

Liquid measures

IMPERIAL	AMERICAN
¼ pint liquid	⅔ cup liquid
½ pint	1¼ cups
¾ pint	2 cups
1 pint	2½ cups
1½ pints	3¾ cups
2 pints	5 cups (2½ pints)

Note: When making any of the recipes in this book, only follow one set of measures as they are not interchangeable.

Foreword

I wrote this meatless cookery book for a number of reasons.
First I wrote it for the countless people I have met who, on learning that I don't eat meat, say: 'I'm not keen on meat either – but how *do* you go about becoming a vegetarian?'
Secondly I wrote it for those people who, also on learning I don't eat meat, always say: 'But what do you *eat*?' in such a manner as to indicate their surprise that I can still stand without the aid of crutches, in spite of the fact that I eschew (as opposed to 'chew') meat.
Thirdly I wrote it for all those existing vegetarians – and there are millions of us all over the world – who would like to expand their culinary capabilities and treat their tastebuds at the same time.

People become vegetarians for many reasons. Some dislike the taste of meat; some think it is healthier to cut down on animal fats; some have doubts about meat technology and the hormones and antibiotics pumped into animals; some think it's wrong and unnecessary to kill animals for food; and some think it is wrong to feed animals cereals and grain, when a good portion of the world's population is starving for want of them.

And more and more people are finding they are *having* to adopt a more vegetarian diet because of the ever increasing cost of meat.

You *can* survive without meat. People have been doing it for thousands of years. Once you start, you will find it's no great sacrifice – in fact, it's surprisingly easy.

My main aim in writing the book was to make it as practical as possible with quick, cheap, appetising and varied everyday meals – plus general advice for the would-be vegetarian. If it helps you to make the transition to a cheaper, healthier meat-free way of life, then I will have succeeded.

Dave Dutton

The Green Revolution Rolls On

Meat is in decline . . .
The Roast Beef of Olde Englande is going out of favour . . .
The 'vegeboom' is on . . .

* In the 1980s there has been an astonishing upsurge in the numbers of people shunning meat as part of their daily diet.
* A Gallup poll conducted in 1986 across mainland Britain discovered that vegetarians represent 2.7% of the population – or around 1½ million people who touch neither flesh, fish nor fowl.
* People no longer eating meat totalled 3.1% of the population – another 1¾ million individuals.
* The combined group of vegetarians and non-meat-eaters therefore totalled 3¼ million people – 1 in 17 of the population.

Over a third of the population said they were eating less meat. The main reason given for this, overall, was on health grounds. The poll, commissioned by the Realeat Company, showed that a third of a million more people had stopped eating meat or become total vegetarians compared with the previous year.

No wonder the meat trade is worried. No wonder the Meat and Livestock Commission decided to spend over £7 million trying to persuade people back to meat.

The main trendsetters among the combined vegetarians and non-meat-eaters are women between the ages of 16 and 24, of whom 12.5% do not eat meat at all. These are the people who, as tomorrow's mothers, cooks and food-buyers, are bound to influence their families towards a healthier vegetarian way of life.

Why are more and more people turning towards vegetarianism?

12

It is plain to see that as the mortality rate from heart disease, strokes, cancer and other degenerative diseases soars, touching almost every family in the land, people are no longer prepared to stand idly by and accept the inevitable. More people are reading the labels on products in the shops and refusing to buy chemically-laden food packed with additives in the form of colourings, flavourings and preservatives. Consumer power has forced manufacturers who want to stay in business to abandon a great many of the additives in favour of healthier alternatives (or even to use none at all).

Exercise and slimming classes abound . . . the NACNE and COMA reports alerted people to the dangers of too much fat, salt and sugar in their diet . . . more people are turning to alternative medicine and away from chemical drugs . . . wholewheat bread and flour are gaining ground over denatured white bread. In short, the public is flexing its muscles.

But why the swing away from meat? Could it be that people are being swayed by newspaper headlines over the past couple of years such as: 'Why meat puts the pressure on your heart', 'Carcinogen found in beef', 'Fresh link between diet and strokes' and 'How safe is the meat you eat?' and by reports like the following?

* Australian researchers from university hospitals in Perth found that when meat-eaters with high blood pressure switched to a vegetarian diet for six weeks, their blood pressure fell significantly during the final week. As soon as they went back on meat, their blood pressure levels soared back to dangerously high levels.
* An Oxford-based study comparing vegetarians with meat-eaters found that the former had lower blood cholesterol – significantly so – than meat-eaters. The vegetarians were slimmer, had a marked reduction in diverticular disease and a lower incidence of gallstones.
* American researchers found indications that substances in beef could cause cancer.
* Dutch scientists reported that deaths from coronary heart disease and cancer fell dramatically with increased fibre intake.

13

* Belgian researcher Dr Jacqueline André claimed that among vegetarians, heart attacks, cerebro-vascular diseases and angina were rarer and the cancer rate was 30% less than among the general meat-eating population. She also reported that vegetarians suffered less from obesity, diabetes, constipation, osteoporosis and kidney stones.

Or could the true 'horror stories' reported in the press be influencing the issue? Witness the following reports:

* Sliced beef advertised as 'traditional roast' had been stewed in a cocktail of additives, flavouring and water and sprayed with brown food paint.
* Nearly 4,000lb of knackers-yard meat contaminated with fecal matter and dirt was intercepted by health officers on its way to hospital and school canteens.
* A court in Bingley, Yorkshire, was told that out of every 100 tins of meat sold, two per cent contained knackers-yard meat, horseflesh or even kangaroo meat.
* Police in County Durham warned that a bullock stolen from a farm had been injected with so many growth hormones that eating the beef in quantity could cause men to grow breasts, affect the growth of children or cause women to sprout beards.
* A National Consumer Council report warned that man-made steaks could contain powdered bone or ground-up hair and canned ham, 38% water.
* Trading standards officers found that a well-known food manufacture's potted chicken mince contained chicken necks and stripped chicken carcasses.
* Sausages contained ground-up snouts, eyeballs and mechanically-recovered meat, dyed pink.
* Knackers-yard meat masqueraded as freshly-killed beef and contained tapeworms and a form of TB.

Growth boosters, antibiotics, insecticides, tenderisers, sometimes even tranquillisers, are some of the hazards meat-eaters risk taking into their bodies. What did the old advertisement say? 'What's meat got – it's got the lot!' Evidently! Add to all this the cruelty of some modern farming methods

14

and it's no wonder that vegetarianism begins to look a wiser, healthier, more humane option.

In 1986, Sainsbury's were forced to close two meat depots at the company's Basingstoke headquarters. The reason? The company's distribution manager said that the public was eating less red meat than *during wartime rationing*.

It's never been easier to become a vegetarian. Every day sees new vegetarian products in the shops. Old attitudes are changing. Even certain members of the royal family are tending towards the vegetarian way of life – giving a lead to others in society. (Perhaps Prince Charles was influenced by his visit to an experimental pig-breeding unit in Warwickshire in 1978. When he saw the conditions the animals were kept under, he remarked: 'I'm glad *I'm* not a pig.') So join the green revolution . . . and vote with your knife and fork!

You Are Not Alone

Quite often, a person thinking of becoming a vegetarian may be put off by the feeling of being an outsider – an oddity almost – in a society that regards eating meat as a convention. They have the idea that they will be quite alone, regarded as a figure of fun and generally left out of things.

True, there are those people who, having been brainwashed into eating meat from an early age, never stop to question the rights and wrongs of the subject.

But more and more in society today, there are people willing to listen to the vegetarian point of view. For the first time, vegetarians are being taken seriously as increasing numbers of people come into contact with vegetarianism, through such factors as more media coverage and the mushrooming in recent years of excellent vegetarian restaurants and eating-houses throughout the country – as well as the increased availability of textured vegetable protein (TVP) meat replacements.

In becoming a vegetarian, you will find you are not on your own. There are vegetarian societies in Great Britain and all over the world. As well as the main Vegetarian Society, there are branches and local societies throughout the country. There are schools, children's homes and homes for the elderly, all catering solely for vegetarians. There are vegetarian and vegan hotels, guest houses and holiday firms. There is a lively vegetarian youth section, with branches in most regions, organising such diverse activities as rock music parties, ice-skating, youth hostel weekends, revue groups, disco nights, visits to vegetarian restaurants, publicity campaigns and overseas visits.

The Vegetarian Society itself publishes a regular magazine (free to members) which keeps you up to date with special articles on nutrition, health, ecology, events and recipes. They also publish an annual International Vegetarian Health-food Handbook which is a directory of vegetarian restaurants, shops, guest houses and hotels throughout the

United Kingdom and the world and contains a useful guide to vegetarian products in the shops.

There are regular cookery courses conducted by experienced members of the Vegetarian Society food and cookery section – ranging from mornings or evenings, to full week-long basic courses. These will provide you with invaluable advice to last you a lifetime.

In addition, the Society can provide you with a wide range of informative leaflets and recipe books, a free information service, provide speakers and cookery demonstrators, and put you in touch with your nearest branch section should you wish to take part in the many social events that take place.

There are some people who dislike joining organisations but if you're becoming a vegetarian, I would say it makes sense to join the Society. You don't *have* to socialise if you don't want to – but the help the Society can give you will be of great benefit, both from a practical point of view and for making you feel *you are not alone*!

The address of the Vegetarian Society UK is Parkdale, Dunham Road, Altrincham, Cheshire WA14 4QG (tel. 061–928 0793).

The Vegetarian Baby

'Is it possible to bring up a baby as a vegetarian?' Of course it is . . . many vegetarian mums and dads have the healthy offspring to prove it.

At the time of writing my three-year-old son Gareth stands a couple of inches taller than most children his age, is brimful with energy (too much sometimes!), bright as a button and a good advert for his mother and father's vegetarian cooking.

Seven pounds 12 oz at birth, he was fed on mother's milk, then soyamilk (not cow's milk), and as he grew older we used the liquidiser to prepare meals . . . progressing to fruit purees, nutmeats, yogurts, mashed banana, macaroni cheese, nut roasts, chopped egg, rice dishes, wholesome home-made soups and bread, pasta, potatoes, lentils, TVP and fresh vegetables.

There are a number of very useful cookbooks written specially for vegetarian babies and toddlers, and the Vegetarian Society will also help with ideas. By giving baby and toddler a vegetarian start in life, you will be ensuring that his young system doesn't have to suffer the toxins that a meat-laden diet would carry.

As usual, it is a question of common-sense in making sure a varied diet is followed, but I would say that the main points to observe are: no cow's milk (or as little as possible in view of the fact that many children seem to develop allergic reactions in the form of eczema and mucus); an additive-free diet as far as possible (this means plenty of home cooking or close inspection of food labels); and not too many sweets.

Have no fears – you are giving your children the best possible start in life.

The Vegetarian Child

I was a vegetarian child.

At school dinners in the 50s, I was faced with unsympathetic teachers who stopped just short of force-feeding me on meat. 'You'll never be a big boy. Look at Johnny – he's eating his pork chop. Come on, get it down you or you're going to be ill' were just some of the comments. Well, I didn't become ill or fade away and my teeth didn't drop out (I haven't needed dental treatment for 30 years).

Although in recent years there has been a better understanding of the vegetarian way of life, I suppose such attitudes still exist in certain members of the teaching profession. They emanate, I suspect, not from a true concern for the child's welfare so much as from an attempt by teachers to inflict their own beliefs on the child. I'm glad to say it didn't work with me . . . nor, I hope, will it change the mind of today's young vegetarian who, whether by reason of compassion or of taste, dislikes the thought of eating dead animal flesh.

Fortunately, help is at hand, as more and more schools are adopting a healthier approach to feeding the young and vegetarian meals appear with greater frequency on school menus.

The purveyors of meat are getting worried. An 'Adopt a Butcher' scheme was started by the meat trade in 1985 to try to persuade children of the dubious 'pleasures' of eating animals. In some places, the idea backfired, as the sight of the deceased beast being chopped up revolted not a few of the children who witnessed the act, probably converting them to vegetarianism for life! Perhaps they hadn't associated the neat little slices of meat on their plates with the sentient creatures which looked out from the fields at the passing school bus.

If a vegetarian child is bothered at school, by either teachers or schoolmates, there are several courses of action that the child or its parents can follow.

What the child can do

* Suggest to the offending teacher that he or she takes the class on a visit to the local slaughterhouse . . . and then see how many of the class change their minds about their meat-eating habits. If the teacher refuses, examine the reasons given . . .
* Put forward the idea of a debate on the pros and cons of vegetarianism, involving the whole class. Do your homework on the subject and anticipate the usual 'anti' arguments.
* Ask the teacher to invite a vegetarian speaker (perhaps a local athlete) to explain why he or she became vegetarian and the benefits he feels he derives from it.
* Point out to schoolmates that meat-eaters (via the feeding of plant foods to cattle, etc.) take the food out of the mouths of other children in under-developed countries.
* Tell schoolmates that scores and scores of their favourite pop and TV stars are vegetarians.

What the parent can do

* Invite the children doing the taunting to a party or a meal at your home and give them a slap-up vegetarian feast. Show them vegetarian eating can be fun. The proof of the pudding . . .
* Make sure your child has an attractive packed lunch to take to school with a variety of fresh vegetarian food.
* Write to the local education authority suggesting more vegetarian meals on the menu.
* Keep a file of newspaper and magazine clippings which point out the beneficial results of being a vegetarian – plus all the horror stories and court cases involving doctored and unfit meat. These can be used as ammunition in your child's classroom debates.
* Above all, the best service any parent can do for a vegetarian child is to ensure that he or she is getting the best vegetarian meals available to give a well-balanced diet and make the child a shining example of the healthy vegetarian way of life.

Footnote: Veggy children take heart. The tide is turning your way. In 1986, when Hampshire Education Council polled schools to find out whether they would like vegetarian meals, they were astounded to find a sixth-form class at a large comprehensive was *entirely* vegetarian; in a village school of 40 pupils there were only five meat-eaters; and in a junior school class, which had done a project on vegetarianism, six months later they *all* ate vegetarian school dinners!

Grow Green

Do you have a spare piece of land at the back of your house? Have you only a tiny garden – or perhaps no garden at all? Whether you have acres of land or only a sunny bedroom window, my advice is the same – don't just sit there, *grow something*!

With farmers spraying pesticides on their crops and ladling chemicals into the ground in which they grow; with fears about irradiated food; it makes good sense to grow your own. Fresh vegetables that go straight from your garden into the pan beat food you buy in the shops hands down on both taste and vitamin content. If you've never tasted peas straight from the pod in your own garden, I feel sorry for you. If you've never discovered the difference between an apple just plucked off the bough and one that has been days, or weeks, on its way to your shopping basket, it will be an eye-opener. And if you remember green beans as a mushy tasteless mess that you used to slide down the back of the radiator in the school canteen, the fresh article will come as a marvellous surprise.

In short, I urge you to do something about growing your own food. If you haven't got a large garden, just grow as much as you can. In my tiny plot, I grow courgettes, broccoli, peas, runner beans, garlic, cabbage, gooseberries, brussels sprouts, leeks, radish and lettuce. A dwarf apple tree provides crisp, mouth-watering apples galore and raspberry canes carry an abundance of fruit.

Even if you live in a flat, you can easily grow something indoors. For a supply of fresh lettuce leaves, a window trough in full sunlight will grow an amazing amount if you choose a dwarf variety such as Tom Thumb. You can grow fresh herbs like parsley, basil or chives with no problems at all. There is even a miniature carrot that you can grow in plant-pots on the windowsill (ask your local garden centre) and the flavour is superb.

If you've time to spare – perhaps retired or unemployed –

ask your local council for an allotment where, for a few pounds' rental a year, you can grow all the fruit and vegetables your family needs. What's the point of sitting indoors when you can be out in the fresh air? You don't have to be an expert. A couple of good gardening books will tell you all you need to know – and there is no shortage of TV advice. If you rent an allotment, you'll be surrounded by experts who will be only too glad to help. For advice on organic gardening, composting and pesticide-free gardening, contact the Soil Association (see Useful Addresses).

Growing your own produce is beneficial in many ways. There's the exercise; there's the wonderful feeling of working hand in glove with nature; there's the subtle enjoyment of doing something positive; but above all you'll have food such as you've never tasted before. So join the green revolution – and *grow-it-yourself*.

Ten Steps Towards Vegetarianism

1 Make the break from meat NOW – not tomorrow or the day after or the day after that! Okay, if you feel that's too drastic, at least give up red meat while you are adjusting your eating habits, and including more and more vegetarian dishes in your daily diet.

2 Make your food your hobby. Go to your local library and study nutrition. Buy yourself a good selection of vegetarian recipe books and look for vegetarian recipes in newspapers and magazines.

3 Plan your meals in advance using the recipes in this and other cookbooks – and your own imagination. If you plan ahead, you'll be less likely to resort to lazy tactics like putting a chop under the grill. Keep a file of all your favourite dishes (perhaps giving them a score system) and use this as part of your meal planner.

4 (One of the most important points). Don't be afraid to experiment – you never know what you're missing until you try. Quite often a vegetarian recipe that looks quite prosaic, and on the face of it unappealing, can turn out to be the opposite. You'll be trying out delicious new types of food that you might never have tried as a meat eater. Think of all the different varieties of fruit, vegetables, rice, eggs, cheese, TVP, pulses, milk, herbs, pastas, cereals and nuts with their variations of colour, taste and texture just waiting for you to experiment with. You'll be surprised at your own capabilities.

5 Think about joining the Vegetarian Society. Find out your nearest local branch and take part in their activities, social events and attend their cookery demonstrations. Swap recipes and hints with vegetarian friends. Show that being a vegetarian isn't the same as being a vegetable.

6 Find out about the new food technology advances. Experiment with TVP meat substitute meals. Find out what you do like about them and what you don't like. Use them with different herbs and flavourings. You hear a lot of meat eaters pooh-poohing TVP, but I know quite a few of them who have eaten TVP and not known the difference.

7 Have a slap-up meal at some of the excellent vegetarian restaurants and eating places that are springing up everywhere. Show you support them. Find one that serves really delicious meals – then take friends along to introduce them to the vegetarian way of life.

8 If you have to eat at work, take along soups, salads, packed lunches – look forward to planning a different lunch every day.

9 With the money you have saved from not having to buy meat, give yourself a break – a new hairdo, sports equipment or a holiday break.

10 Remember that, by your example, other people may be persuaded to take up vegetarianism. So always look your best, keep healthy – and smile! Here's to many hours of happy, healthy eating.

What to Swap

A guide to help those becoming vegetarians to replace animal-based products with those of a vegetarian nature.

Minced beef Replace with loose TVP (textured vegetable protein) available from most health-food shops. The loose TVP is usually a lot cheaper than packet TVP. See the section on TVP.

Bacon flavour Addicts can satisfy their craving for a smoky bacon flavour by buying Smokey Snaps. Use as directed.

Ham/chicken flavour Soya-derived substitutes are available at health shops – though how close they taste to the original will have to be decided by the individual. Personally, I avoid.

Sausages Replace with the excellent brands of sausage substitutes such as Sosmix or VegeBanger. These can also be used in sausage rolls (making sure the puff pastry is made with vegetable oil). Add your own flavourings, if you wish, to the sausage mixture – tomato puree or pepper or a herb of your fancy such as basil. Experiment.

Burgers Burgamix is excellent – as is VegeBurger. Make up as directed and serve on a bap or burger bun with fried onions on a bed of lettuce. Great for children's parties, barbecues, etc. Realeat's ready-made VegeBurgers save time.

Lard Use vegetarian margarines or cooking oils such as corn oil.

Cheese There is a range of vegetarian cheeses available which do not contain any rennet (an extract from the stomach of unweaned calves containing the enzyme rennin, used for clotting the milk.) Singleton's of Longridge, near Preston, have used vegetarian rennet for 200 years. You can also obtain cheese made from rennet-free soya, made in Sweden and distributed by Kallo Foods. Soderasens cheese is made from vegetable oil and skimmed milk.

Milk Can, if you wish, be replaced by soya milk. Use slightly chilled over breakfast cereals. Children will enjoy the flavoured varieties such as strawberry, carob or coconut – available in health-food shops and supermarkets. I would urge you to replace the majority of your cow's milk intake with soya milk (it's cholesterol free) – perhaps using the former only in tea or coffee.

Jelly The usual kind is based on gelatine made from the bones, hooves and hides of animals (a pleasant thing to give your children!) and colourings. Use agar agar or similar (ask at your health-food shop) in recipes. Or for a ready-made range of desserts try the Mr Merry jellies which have no gelatine, starch, artificial colourings, preservatives or animal ingredients.

Gravy See vegetarian gravy recipe on page 62. It may surprise you that Bisto gravy is vegetarian (in packet form). The granules are not (check label).

Stuffing If you like the taste of stuffing (in nut roasts etc.), vegetarian stuffing is available from health-food shops.

Haggis Believe it or not, for those Scottish vegetarians (and others) who couldn't possibly face Burns Night or Hogmanay without a haggis on the plate, you can obtain a vegetarian version from Macsweens of Edinburgh, 130 Bruntsfield Place, Edinburgh EH10 4ES (tel. 031–229 1216). Pick one up from the shop – or they will post you one! Telephone for current prices.

Beef extracts, Bovril, etc. Use Vecon, Marmite, Yeastrel, Barmene, etc. These are yeast extracts excellent for making stock (especially Vecon), gravies, sauces and spreads. Rich in B vitamins (some contain B_{12} too – check label).

Cold meats Use canned nutmeat, sliced.

Suets Replace with nut suets.

Pâtés, spreads Use Tartex – a very tasty spread available at most healthfood shops. Granose, Duchesse and Sunwheel do a variety of spreads.

Fritters, rissoles etc. Many savoury mixtures available.

27

Worcestershire sauce Buy an anchovy-free variety. Try 'Life'.

Ice cream Frequently contains animal ingredients. America has long enjoyed a soya-based substitute which is becoming more widely available over here.

Cookery magazines Ask your local newsagent to stock *The Vegetarian* or *Green Cuisine* (an excellent high-class publication containing vegetarian recipes, the latest advances in vegetarian foods, helpful advice – all extremely well presented).

Points to watch out for Always look at labels when shopping. You may come across lentil soup with beef fat in it; 'shortening' in convenience foods might mean animal fat; lots of biscuits contain animal fat; so do some pizzas and some bread. Even margarine may contain fish oils, so do check. Use a margarine without colourings and animal fats – DP Pure by S. D. Matthews Ltd., Ossett, West Yorkshire, is ideal for vegetarians and vegans and is very reasonably priced. Use your consumer power. If you want organically-grown vegetables, animal-free products, vegetarian convenience foods, soya milk, etc., ask your local supermarket manager to stock it. He won't know the demand if you don't ask. Enlightened food chains such as Sainsbury's, Marks and Spencer and Boots already take this approach. Three and a quarter million vegetarians and non-meat-eaters represent a large and ever-growing market.

A–Z Guide to Vegetarianism

Additives Some foodstuffs might appear on the face of it to be vegetarian but may in fact have contents of animal origin. Always check the label or consult the Vegetarian Society's International Handbook.

Airlines Will generally cater for vegetarian travellers – *given prior warning.* (The meals are often better than the ones you would normally get.)

Anti-blood sports Many vegetarians are anti-blood sports. There are addresses of anti-blood sport organisations in the list of Useful Addresses (see page 207).

Athletes You don't have to eat meat to excel at sport – vegetarians have an excellent track record when it comes to sporting achievements. Vegetarian sportsmen have won Olympic gold medals for running, weightlifting and swimming, and there have been vegetarian world and European boxing champions. Vegetarians have also excelled in the fields of cross-channel swimming, cycling and long-distance walking – all demanding great stamina and endurance.

B 12 A vitamin not generally found in plant food and so may be of some concern to people contemplating becoming vegetarian or vegan. However, deficiency in it is unlikely, unless you avoid dairy produce or eggs. It has been said that lack of this vitamin can lead to pernicious anaemia, but nowadays B 12 is added to yeast extracts and some textured vegetable protein. Or you can easily obtain it in supplements.

Babies Feeding babies a vegetarian diet is no problem – as generations of healthy vegetarians have proved. There are several books on the subject and the Vegetarian Society is able to provide advice to the vegetarian mother. A list of manufactured vegetarian infant foods and cereals can be found in the Society's handbook – but it is quite easy to make your own purées, cereals or juices for baby.

Beauty Without Cruelty This is an international organisation promoting and supplying natural cosmetics, in which no animal products are found. You will find Beauty Without Cruelty address in Useful Addresses (see page 207).

Camreb The Campaign for Real Bread is an organisation which advocates the use of wholewheat bread in place of denaturalised plasticky white bread, on the grounds that wholewheat bread is tastier, healthier and contains less chemicals. The Vegetarian Society will pass on your letters if you wish to support this cause.

Cheese Vegetarian cheese is available in health food shops and some larger supermarkets. Vegans do not eat cheese.

Cholesterol Although this substance, possibly connected to heart disease, is found in fatty meats, cold cooked meats, sausages, shellfish, duck and offal, don't think that by becoming a vegetarian you automatically embark on a low-cholesterol diet. True, you will have a head start over most meat eaters, but cholesterol is also found in milk, full-fat cheeses, egg yolks, chocolate, omelettes cooked in butter, flaky pastries and mayonnaise. It's up to you whether you want to cut down your intake of these foodstuffs.

Always use margarines labelled 'high in polyunsaturates'. Where recipes include butter, these margarines can be used – it's entirely up to you. If you want to lower your cholesterol intake even further, use low-fat products such as cottage cheese, Edam cheese and skimmed milk. Use a good corn oil for cooking or making dressings.

Keeping your eye on your cholesterol intake is a matter of common-sense – and not a springboard for a neurosis.

Dieters and slimmers can obtain leaflets and advice from the Vegetarian Society.

Eggs Ovo-lacto vegetarians eat eggs but vegans do not. Free range eggs are preferred.

Elderly vegetarians There are homes for elderly vegetarians in several parts of the country and enquiries should be made to the Vegetarian Society in London.

Fibre By eating more plant food, you are taking in more fibre and this helps towards alleviating that great British preoccupation – constipation. I can honestly say I have never once been afflicted by it since becoming a vegetarian. There is increasing feeling that certain illnesses and diseases of the intestines might be avoided by including more fibre in the diet – another 'plus' in favour of vegetarianism.

Food poisoning A bonus to vegetarians and vegans is that they are less likely to get food poisoning than meat eaters, as over 90 per cent of cases of food poisoning are due to meat.

Food reform Food reformers are not necessarily vegetarians. They shun devitalised foods, such as white flour, white sugar and white rice, replacing them with wholefoods such as brown unpolished rice, stone-ground wholewheat flour and molasses, etc. They eat lots of fresh fruit and vegetables – avoiding canned and processed foods. They keep down to a minimum the stodgy food such as cakes, puddings and biscuits.

Get fit! Becoming a vegetarian doesn't automatically confer great health and fitness upon anyone. You still have to work at maintaining a reasonable level of fitness by doing some exercise every day.

Holidays These can be a slight problem if you don't fancy self-catering. Get your travel agent to check whether the holiday firm can provide vegetarian meals. Then double check with the hotel and always give lots of prior warning. Always thank the firm and the hotel concerned if all goes well.

Hospitals The Department of Health and Social Security recognise that vegetarian meals should be provided on request in hospitals. Again, give the hospital plenty of prior notice and enquire whether they need further advice regarding recipes, etc. Be co-operative, thankful and polite.

Herbs Experiment with fresh herbs in your food. It's healthy and it's fun.

Indian restaurants These are a very good place to find a wide selection of vegetarian meals, if you enjoy eating out.

Jail If you ever find yourself in prison, you can be provided with vegetarian food on request!

Kith and kin They can be gently introduced to meatless meals by letting them sample delicious vegetarian fare. If they enjoy it, let them have the recipe.

Live and let live The motto of the vegetarian movement – and a good way to run your life.

Milk Milk is something which vegans do not drink. Plant milk can now be bought in most health food stores and can be used in place of cow's milk.

Molasses This is an excellent food containing lots of minerals and is rich in iron and calcium. It is best bought unsulphured.

Nuts Walnuts, brazils, cashews, almonds, hazelnuts and peanuts (strictly speaking, a legume) are another valuable source of protein. Peanuts contain the highest concentration of protein at 30 per cent, followed by almonds (21 per cent), walnuts (18 per cent), brazils (17 per cent), cashews (12 per cent) and hazelnuts (9 per cent).

Nuts should be eaten regularly, although sparingly, as they are high in calories. They can be used in nut roasts and muesli (see pages 61 and 185). You can also make your own nut spreads, by finely grinding a handful of nuts and combining with margarine, salt, pepper and fresh herbs to taste. Spread on wholemeal bread. Cashew nuts and peanuts are delicious when roasted lightly and sprinkled over salads.

Nutmeat, available in cans from health food stores, is a tasty addition when sliced and added to salads or used in sandwiches. Nut rissole mixtures can also be bought from health food shops.

Obligations If you become a vegetarian, you have obligations to your fellow vegetarians. *Don't* go about with a holier-than-thou attitude, especially when in company with meat eaters. *Don't* be dogmatic or over-assertive towards people regarding your belief in vegetarianism. You'll be doing the movement a disservice and nobody likes a bore, anyway. *Do* set an example by trying to keep as fit, slim and healthy as possible by exercising regularly and eating a balanced diet.

Overseas readers See page 36.

Pets There's no reason why cats and dogs can't be vegetarian too. Get advice from the Vegetarian Society on how to go about it.

Pulses This is a blanket name for peas, beans and lentils. They are a good source of protein, though incomplete unless combined with grains or cereals (as in beans on wholemeal toast). Being dry, they store well.

All pulses benefit from soaking before cooking – beans should be soaked overnight and peas and lentils for 4–6 hours. Soya beans take the longest to cook – about 3–4 hours; other beans take from 1–2 hours and peas and lentils take about 30–45 minutes.

Among the pulses are haricot beans, mung beans, butter beans, black-eyed beans, chick peas, peas, aduki beans, lentils, yellow and green split peas and, of course, the protein-packed soya bean.

Queries If you have any queries about becoming a vegetarian, the Vegetarian Society will be glad to help you (but don't forget to include a couple of stamps for postage).

Restaurants Don't put up with omelettes all the time. Ring the restaurant to ask if they can serve vegetarian meals or see the Vegetarian Society's handbook for a list of vegetarian restaurants throughout the United Kingdom and the world.

Schoolchildren See page 19.

Soil Association This is a society founded by people from all walks of life, who believe that organic farming and gardening is the best method to make the soil more fertile, thus producing better crops of a higher nutritional value, leading to better health. They are against the use of chemicals, insecticides and pesticides on the soil and promote ways of replacing these methods with natural organic ones. (See Useful Addresses on page 207.)

Tips Always read the small type on the side of food packages, and try to avoid things with too many chemicals, additives and preservatives.

Vegans Vegans take vegetarianism one step further and do not eat meat, fish, honey, dairy products or eggs. The Society was founded in 1944 and advocates living on the products of the plant kingdom, to the exclusion of all food and other commodities derived from animals.

They believe that animal products are unnecessary for human health and that it is possible to rear happy, healthy intelligent families and to live full and active lives to a vigorous old age on plant products.

Vegans believe that Western feeding habits (and thus Western diseases) are spreading through the affluent classes of the developing countries – thus exacerbating the situation of the poor. (See Useful Addresses on page 207.)

Wholefood buying You can sometimes save a lot of money by buying wholefoods in bulk.

You'll be in good company if you become a vegetarian. You might have heard vegetarians described as cranks, but Leonardo da Vinci, Plato, Tolstoy, Ovid, Voltaire, Gandhi,

34

Pythagoras, Socrates, Plutarch, Milton, Shelley, Sir Isaac Newton and George Bernard Shaw were vegetarians. *These* were cranks? Not forgetting some of the world's strongest animals – the elephant, gorilla, bull, horse – which are all vegetarians.

Z Stands for *zest*, something I hope you'll get more of by becoming a vegetarian, and following the recipes in this book!

NOTE FOR OVERSEAS READERS

This is where I extend greetings to vegetarian (and would-be vegetarian) readers across the sea. As you make the change to a new way of life, it is reassuring to know that there are among your fellow countrymen and women lots of people who think as you do. There are vegetarian societies all over the world simply waiting for you to contact them to give you their help and advice, gained over many years of experience of vegetarianism. Here are some contacts:

For American and Canadian readers, North America is well served with numerous vegetarian societies from Florida to Philadelphia, from Milwaukee to Maine. There is even a Vegetarian Information Service in Texas! Canada has societies in both Toronto and Calgary – vegetarians in the heart of cattle country. Great!

The co-ordinating body in Canada and America, representing nearly 60 affiliated local groups is: The North American Vegetarian Society, 501, Old Harding Highway, Malaga, New Jersey 08328 (Telephone (609) 694–2887).

They will advise you of your nearest vegetarian or animal protection society. You may also join them and receive the *Vegetarian Voice* magazine, containing recipes, news and features on vegetarian topics, several times a year. They will also give you help in starting a vegetarian society in your area.

The Society works full time, year round, to educate the public and interested organisations in the values of vegetarianism. They also foster respect for the environment and kindness to living creatures. Readers in the USA and Canada should contact the Society, enclosing a stamped addressed envelope where possible.

Another useful address for American readers is the Vegetarian Information Service, Box 5888, Washington D.C. 20014. They provide information on all aspects of vegetarianism from diets for dogs and cats to infant feeding and the well-being of the elderly.

For New Zealand readers, contact the New Zealand

Vegetarian Society Inc, at PO Box 454, Auckland, New Zealand.

The secretary, Mrs L. MacIntyre, writes: 'The group is very active, particularly in Auckland, and takes part in demonstrations and street stalls whenever the opportunity arises. Auckland branch have monthly meetings on the last Thursday of every month and there are also branches in all the main centres of New Zealand, including Wellington.'

The Society also puts out quarterly newsletters which are sent free to members, and they run a postal library service and also sell books on vegetarianism. Contact telephone – Mrs L. MacIntyre, (Auckland) 543–977.

For South African readers, there are societies in Cape Town, Johannesburg and Natal. Contact: The South African Vegetarian Union, PO Box 23601, Joubert Park 2044 TVL (Telephone 664–2936).

For Australian readers, your contact is: The Vegetarian Society of Australasia, 723 Glenhuntly Road, S. Caulfield, Victoria 3162.

Other overseas readers may check their Vegetarian Society address through health food shops or the telephone directory.

Soups and Starters

'*Soup of the evening, beautiful soup!*' Lewis Carroll (*Alice in Wonderland*).

There is something about a good soup that seems to permeate warmth and nourishment to every recess of your body. What could be more welcoming on a cold winter's night than a hot bowlful of soup, sizzling with crunchy croûtons or served with a chunk of crusty French bread?

Soups, by their very nature, lend themselves to experimentation with all manner of vegetables, herbs and spices. To me, half the fun of making soup is adding a pinch of this and a dash of that to achieve new flavours to tickle the tastebuds.

When I worked as a reporter, I once visited an old man who told me that neither fish, flesh nor fowl had passed his lips since he was a young man. He was in his 70s, ramrod-straight and looking 20 years younger with a full head of hair and a strong confident voice. While talking to him, a delicious smell wafted from the kitchen. On enquiry, he told me it was the vegetable stockpot which he kept going every day in order to make himself soups.

He remained fit and active well into his 90s – walking without the aid of a stick. He was a grand advertisement for the vegetarian way of life.

Now I'm not suggesting that his soup was some magic elixir, but when you consider that your body needs lots of vitamins, minerals and salts to regenerate its cells, a good bowlful of fresh, home-made soup must go a long way to providing that nourishment.

The secret of a soup that tastes good and does you good is to start with a good stock.

TAKING STOCK

Stock can be made with almost everything in the way of vegetables: leaves and stalks of greens, carrots, celery, lettuce,

38

stalks of cauliflowers, etc. Just put them into a saucepan containing a couple of pints of water, boil, then simmer for a couple of hours. Strain, throw away the vegetables – and there you have stock.

A quick vegetarian stock can be made by stirring a couple of tablespoonfuls of Vecon into warm water. It also contains vitamin B_{12}.

Never throw away the water in which you have boiled vegetables – use it as the basis of stock.

Note: A liquidiser is extremely handy for speeding up the time taken to make soup.

I have included starters at the end of this chapter. You can use some of the salad recipes as first courses, too.

MIXED VEGETABLE SOUP
Cooking time 40 minutes
SERVES 4–6

1 onion, finely chopped	1 carrot
40 g/1½ oz margarine	3 tablespoons mixed cereals
2 sticks of celery	and pulses
1 leek	1 clove garlic, finely
1 medium potato	chopped
salt and black pepper	½ teaspoon yeast extract
1.15 litres/2 pints stock or	pinch mixed herbs
water	1 bay leaf

Fry the onion in the margarine in a large pan for a few minutes. Chop the celery, leek and potato into small pieces and add to the onion. Heat together for 2–3 minutes to extract the flavour – keeping the lid on the pan and making sure the ingredients don't stick. Add salt and pepper. Pour in the stock and stir well. Chop the carrot into small pieces and add. Then add the washed cereals and pulses, garlic, yeast extract, herbs, bay leaf and more salt and pepper to taste. Stir well and cook over a low heat for 20–30 minutes.

POTATO, LEEK AND CELERY SOUP
Cooking time about 30 minutes
SERVES 4–6

1 small onion, finely
  chopped
40 g/1½ oz margarine
2 medium potatoes
2 leeks

1 head of celery
salt and black pepper
1.15 litres/2 pints stock
pinch garlic salt
about 3 tablespoons milk

Cook the onion in the margarine in a pan for a few minutes.
Chop the potatoes, leeks and celery into small pieces, add to
the onion with some salt and pepper. Simmer for a few
minutes with lid on. Add the stock, garlic salt and more salt
and pepper to taste. Stir well and simmer until cooked. Add
a little milk just before serving.

This soup is delicious if liquidised (after allowing to cool),
then returned to the pan for a few minutes to heat gently,
adding a little milk.

CARROT AND ORANGE SOUP
Cooking time about 30 minutes
SERVES 4

2 medium onions
grated rind of 1 large orange
25 g/1 oz butter
450 g/1 lb carrots, sliced

900 ml/1½ pints stock
juice of 2 large oranges
salt and black pepper

Cook the onions and grated orange rind in the butter for a
few minutes in a covered pan. Add the carrots and stock and
simmer, covered, for 15 minutes. Allow to cool slightly and
then blend in a liquidiser until smooth. Add the orange juice
and blend again. Return to the saucepan to reheat, then season
and serve.

ALFALFA TOMATO SOUP
Cooking time about 20 minutes
SERVES 4

5 large tomatoes, skinned
   and chopped
½ bay leaf
pinch thyme
2 cloves
2 thin slices of onion
25 g/1 oz margarine

600 ml/1 pint water
1 tablespoon cornflour
½ teaspoon salt
25 g/1 oz alfalfa sprouts (see
   page 138)
4 tablespoons grated
   Parmesan

Put the tomatoes, herbs, cloves, onion and margarine in a pan and cook over a low heat for 10 minutes. Remove the cloves and bay leaf. Press the tomato mixture through a sieve or liquidise. Add the water and cornflour mixed, stir well and cook until slightly thickened. Add the salt and alfalfa sprouts and reheat. Serve hot, topping each serving with a sprinkling of grated Parmesan.

ONION SOUP
Cooking time 40 minutes
SERVES 4–5

450 g/1 lb potatoes
50 g/2 oz margarine
3 large onions, chopped
750 ml/1¼ pints water

salt and pepper
150 ml/¼ pint milk
chopped fresh parsley

Dice the potatoes. Melt the margarine and add the potatoes and onions. Cook over a low heat, shaking the pan occasionally. After a few minutes, pour on the water and continue to cook over a low heat for 30 minutes. Add the salt and pepper and, just before serving, stir in the milk and a little chopped parsley. You may also add a little single cream, if liked.

LEEK AND LENTIL SOUP
Cooking time 1 hour 15 minutes
SERVES 4–6

100 g/4 oz lentils
1.75 litres/3 pints stock or
  water
1 stick of celery
1 small onion
1 large leek

40 g/1½ oz margarine
25 g/1 oz flour
300 ml/½ pint milk
1 teaspoon salt
1 teaspoon yeast extract

Thoroughly wash the lentils, then place in the stock or water and bring to the boil. When boiling, add the vegetables, cut into small pieces, then simmer for about 1 hour until tender. Press through a sieve.

Put the margarine and flour in a large pan and stir together over a low heat. Gradually stir in the milk, then add the soup, salt and yeast extract. Bring to the boil, stirring, simmer a few more minutes, then serve.

CAULIFLOWER CHEESY SNOW SOUP
Cooking time 40 minutes
SERVES 4–5

1 large onion
5 large sticks of celery
25 g/1 oz margarine
900 ml/1½ pints stock
1 small head of cauliflower,
  broken into florets
5 tablespoons millet, washed
  (optional)

celery salt
onion salt
garlic salt
150 ml/¼ pint milk
salt and pepper
crumbly cheese such as
  Lancashire

Roughly chop the onion and celery and fry gently in the margarine with the lid on the pan. When soft, pour on the stock and cauliflower florets. Add the millet, bring to the boil and simmer for 20 minutes, adding a generous pinch each of celery, onion and garlic salts.

Let the soup cool, then liquidise and return to the pan. Stir in the milk and salt and pepper to taste. Heat slowly until ready to serve. Sprinkle a generous amount of crumbly cheese over each individual serving.

RED WARMER
Cooking time 55 minutes
SERVES 4–6

1 medium onion	1.15 litres/2 pints stock
2 sticks of celery (optional)	225 g/8 oz carrots, sliced
25 g/1 oz margarine	100 g/4 oz lentils, washed
pinch garlic salt	salt and black pepper

Roughly chop the onion and celery. Melt the margarine in a pan, add the onion, celery, garlic salt and fry until soft. Add the stock, carrots and lentils. Bring to the boil, and simmer for 30–40 minutes or until the carrots are just cooked.

Allow to cool, then liquidise and return to the pan, adding salt and pepper to taste. Reheat and serve in individual bowls with hot croûtons (see page 50).

Note: This is a very filling soup.

JAPANESE MISO SOUP

Miso is a traditional Japanese food. It is made by a long natural fermentation of soya beans, sea salt and water and can be used as a base for soups, or as an addition to gravies, casseroles, stews and pies. The Japanese people eat miso soup for breakfast and it is said to cleanse poisons from the blood.

Cooking time 30 minutes
SERVES 4–6

1 medium onion, roughly chopped	2 strips wakame seaweed
	pinch garlic salt
3 carrots, diced	3 tablespoons miso
3 cabbage leaves, chopped	black pepper
40 g/1½ oz margarine	
1.15 litres/2 pints boiling water	

Gently fry the onion, carrots and cabbage leaves in the margarine. Add the boiling water, wakame and garlic salt, then simmer until the vegetables are cooked.

Dilute the miso in a small quantity of warm water and stir until a smooth consistency is achieved. Pour into the vegetables, stir well, turn off the heat and allow the miso to mingle. Add the black pepper and serve while still hot.

Note: An important point to remember in this recipe is not to boil the miso, as this destroys useful enzymes inherent in the purée. Miso is available in wholefood and health food shops. You can also use any vegetables you like in this recipe.

GREEN SPLIT PEA AND MISO SOUP
Cooking time about 1 hour 15 minutes
SERVES 4–6

225 g/8 oz green split peas	½ teaspoon mixed herbs
600 ml/1 pint water	bay leaf
1 medium onion	salt and pepper
1 carrot	1½ tablespoons miso
2 large sticks of celery	fresh or dried marjoram to
40 g/1½ oz margarine	garnish
600 ml/1 pint stock	

Soak the peas overnight, or for a few hours, in the water. Thinly slice the onion, carrot and celery and gently cook in the margarine with the pan lid on for 10–15 minutes. Shake the pan to prevent the vegetables sticking. Then add the split peas, with the water they have been soaking in, the stock, herbs and bay leaf. Bring to boil, cover and simmer for 45 minutes to 1 hour until the peas are soft. Remove the bay leaf. Allow to cool, then liquidise and return to the pan. Add seasoning to taste.

When the soup is reheating, take a cupful of the soup and stir in the miso until thoroughly dissolved. Pour the miso liquid into the soup and stir well. Reheat the soup, but *do not allow to boil.* Serve with marjoram to garnish and hot croûtons (see page 50) if liked.

CHEDDAR SOUP
Cooking time 15–20 minutes
SERVES 4

1 medium onion
40 g/1½ oz margarine
25 g/1 oz flour
600 ml/1 pint milk
300 ml/½ pint water or
  stock
salt and pepper

small pinch cayenne pepper
bay leaf
175 g/6 oz Cheddar cheese,
  grated
fresh or dried marjoram to
  garnish

Finely chop the onion and fry gently in the margarine until soft but still white. Add the flour and cook for 1 minute, stirring. Stir in the milk, water or stock, salt, pepper and cayenne pepper. Add the bay leaf and simmer gently for 5–7 minutes.

Remove the bay leaf. Take the pan from the heat and stir in the Cheddar cheese. Serve immediately, with a sprinkling of marjoram and hot croûtons (see page 50).

WATERCRESS SOUP
Cooking time 30 minutes
SERVES 4–5

1 medium onion
25 g/1 oz margarine
2 bunches watercress,
  roughly chopped
2 medium potatoes

600 ml/1 pint stock
300 ml/½ pint milk
salt and pepper
150 ml/¼ pint soured cream

Slice the onion and fry gently in the margarine. Add most of the watercress, reserving a little for garnish, thin sliced potatoes, stock, milk and seasoning. Simmer for 20 minutes, then cool and liquidise. Add the soured cream and reheat gently. Garnish with the reserved chopped watercress.

45

CREAMY POTATO SOUP
Cooking time about 35 minutes
SERVES 4–6

1 large onion
2–3 sticks of celery
1 clove garlic, finely
  chopped
40 g/1½ oz margarine
3–4 large potatoes
900 ml/1½ pints stock

celery salt
salt and pepper
bay leaf
2 tablespoons flour
300 ml/½ pint milk
chopped chives or cooked
  garden peas

Roughly chop the onion and celery. Fry them together with the garlic in the margarine, making sure they don't stick to the pan.

Slice the potatoes and add to the pan, with the stock, celery salt, salt and pepper and bay leaf. Simmer until the potatoes are soft, then allow to cool. Remove the bay leaf and liquidise or press through a sieve.

Mix the flour thoroughly with the warmed milk, add to the soup and gently reheat but do not boil. Add the salt and pepper. To give colour and extra nourishment, add some chopped chives or cooked garden peas. Serve with hot croûtons (see page 50).

Note: For a thicker soup, 5 tablespoons double cream may be added after the milk.

CREAMY BARLEY SOUP
Cooking time about 2 hours
SERVES 4

100 g/4 oz pearl barley
900 ml/1½ pints stock
25 g/1 oz margarine

150 ml/¼ pint double cream
salt and pepper

Add the pearl barley to the stock and bring to boil. Simmer gently for 1½–2 hours or until the barley is soft. Retain 2–3 tablespoons of the cooked barley, then pour the rest through a sieve. Return the barley liquid to the pan, together with the 2–3 tablespoons barley. Stir in the milk, margarine, cream and salt and pepper. Heat and serve.

HARVEST SOUP
Cooking time 50 minutes
SERVES 4–6

450 g/1 lb carrots, diced
225 g/8 oz potatoes, diced
1 medium onion, finely
  chopped
25 g/1 oz margarine
450 ml/¾ pint stock
50 g/2 oz lentils

salt and black pepper
25 g/1 oz flour
600 ml/1 pint milk
100 g/4 oz Cheddar cheese,
  grated
cooked garden peas and
  croûtons to garnish

Gently fry the carrots, potatoes and onion in the margarine for 5 minutes, then add the stock, lentils, salt and black pepper. Bring to the boil, then simmer for 30 minutes.

Mix the flour with some of the milk and add to the soup, then add the remaining milk, stirring all the time. Gently simmer for a further 5 minutes, then stir in 75 g/3 oz of the Cheddar cheese. Serve immediately, sprinkled with the rest of the cheese, cooked garden peas and croûtons (see page 50).

BRUSSELS SPROUTS SOUP
Cooking time about 30 minutes
SERVES 4–6

1 medium onion, finely
  chopped
40 g/1½ oz margarine
1.15 litres/2 pints stock
1 medium potato, sliced
450 g/1 lb Brussels sprouts

½ teaspoon yeast extract
pinch garlic salt
pinch celery salt
salt and pepper
top of the milk

Fry the onion in the margarine until soft and white. Pour on the stock and add the sliced potato, Brussels sprouts, yeast extract, garlic and celery salt. Bring to the boil and simmer with the lid on until the Brussels sprouts are well cooked. Allow to cool, then liquidise. Return to the pan, reheat and add the seasoning. Stir in the top of the milk just before serving.

47

CREAMY TOMATO SOUP

Cooking time 35 minutes

SERVES 4

1 kg/2 lb ripe tomatoes
300 ml/½ pint water
1 teaspoon salt
2 teaspoons sugar
black pepper

50 g/2 oz margarine
25 g/1 oz flour
450 ml/¾ pint creamy milk
chopped fresh parsley and
   basil to garnish

Cut the tomatoes into quarters, removing the hard centres at the top. Put in a pan with the water, then add the salt, sugar and black pepper. Bring to the boil, then simmer very gently with the pan lid on for 10–15 minutes. When soft, press the tomatoes through a fine sieve, discarding the skins and pips.

Melt the margarine in a pan and stir in the flour to make a smooth paste. Add the milk, stirring to prevent lumps forming. Gradually add the tomato mixture, stirring all the time until nearly boiling but do not allow to boil. Adjust the seasoning and sprinkle chopped parsley and basil on top of each individual bowl. Serve with hot croûtons (see page 50).

BROCCOLI AND GARDEN PEA SOUP

Cooking time 30 minutes

SERVES 4–6

1 medium onion, chopped
1 large stick of celery,
   chopped
25 g/1 oz margarine
1.15 litres/2 pints stock
1 medium potato, thinly
   sliced
225 g/8 oz broccoli, broken
   into florets
100 g/4 oz garden peas

½ teaspoon yeast extract
1 bay leaf
½ teaspoon chopped fresh
   parsley
½ teaspoon celery salt
salt and pepper
single cream or top of the
   milk
marjoram to garnish

Fry the onion and celery gently in the margarine until soft. Add the stock to the pan with the potato, broccoli and peas.

Next add the yeast extract, bay leaf, parsley and celery salt, stir well and bring to the boil. Simmer with lid on, stirring occasionally, until the vegetables are soft. Remove the bay leaf.

Cool, then sieve or liquidise and return to the pan. Adjust the seasoning. Reheat the soup and serve in individual bowls topped with a decorative whirl of cream or top of the milk and a small pinch of marjoram.

LINDA McCARTNEY'S GREEN PEA SOUP

This is a special recipe kindly given to me by Linda McCartney, wife of Paul McCartney, of the group 'Wings'. The McCartney family are entirely vegetarian and are a healthy advert for the vegetarian way of life. Here then is Linda's family-size recipe for green pea soup:

Cooking time 2–3 hours

SERVES 4

450 g/1 lb green split peas (soaked overnight)	4 tomatoes, skinned
	4 leeks, chopped
225 g/8 oz lentils	butter
3 large onions, quartered	few peppercorns, crushed
1 head of celery, including leaves, roughly chopped	sprinkling of sea salt

Put the split peas, lentils, onions, celery, tomatoes and leeks in a pan and cover with water. Simmer until soft – about 2–3 hours. When ready, add a large knob of butter, some crushed peppercorns and sea salt to taste. Stir and serve.

PEA SOUP
Cooking time 35 minutes
SERVES 4

1 small leek
some shredded lettuce
75 g/3 oz margarine
300 ml/½ pint water
450 g/1 lb fresh or frozen
  garden peas

sprig of mint
450 ml/¾ pint milk
pinch salt
pinch sugar
150 ml/¼ pint single cream

Chop the leek and cook with the lettuce in 50 g/2 oz margarine. Add the water, peas, mint and cook until tender. Liquidise or press through a sieve. Add milk to the required consistency and season. Blend in the cream and the rest of the margarine. Heat gently for a few minutes, then serve.

LIGHTNING PEA SOUP

1 425-g/15-oz can green peas
salt and pepper
pinch castor sugar

about 300 ml/½ pint milk
mint

Blend the peas in a liquidiser for a few seconds. Add the seasoning, castor sugar, mint and milk to required consistency. Heat until ready to serve. Top with croûtons (see below).

To make croûtons (If you know what croûtons are, ignore this bit.) If you don't know what croûtons are, read on. They are thick slices of bread, with crusts removed, cut into dice. The bread cubes are then fried in butter or margarine (with a little garlic added, if liked) until golden brown. To serve, drop croûtons, sizzling hot, into any soup. They are fattening but crunchy and delicious.

LENTIL AND CARROT SOUP
Cooking time about 1 hour 10 minutes
SERVES 4

1 large onion, roughly
  chopped
2 cloves garlic, finely
  chopped
40 g/1½ oz margarine

900 ml/1½ pints stock
175 g/6 oz lentils (red)
450 g/1 lb carrots
salt and white pepper.

Fry the onion and garlic gently in the margarine for a few minutes until soft. Add stock, lentils and sliced carrots. Bring to the boil, then simmer for about an hour until the carrots are cooked. Allow to cool, then liquidise and return to pan. Season and reheat.

Note: Before cooking the lentils, pick over to remove stones and husks, then wash thoroughly in several changes of water.

FRENCH–STYLE ONION SOUP
Cooking time 35 minutes
SERVES 4

2 large onions
2 cloves garlic, finely
  chopped
40 g/1½ oz margarine
900 ml/1½ pints stock
1 tablespoon unbleached
  white flour

5 tablespoons yeast extract
  (such as Marmite)
fresh black pepper
1 bay leaf

Peel and slice the onions thinly (but not *too* thinly). Melt the margarine in a saucepan and fry the sliced onions gently in the covered pan for 15–20 minutes. Stir to prevent sticking. When the onions are soft, stir in the flour, then add the stock and yeast extract, stirring all the time. Bring to the boil, then simmer very gently for 15 minutes with bay leaf. Add lots of black pepper to taste. You won't need any salt as the yeast extract contains plenty. If you wish, you can add a dash or two of soy sauce. Remove bay leaf and serve with crusty French bread.

CELERY SOUP
Cooking time about 50 minutes
SERVES 3–4

40 g/1½ oz margarine
1 medium onion, rough-
  chopped
1 clove garlic, chopped
2 tablespoons flour
750 ml/1¼ pints stock

2 heads of celery weighing
  about 350 g/12 oz
salt and white pepper
150 ml/¼ pint milk
pinch nutmeg

Melt the margarine in a large saucepan and fry the onion and garlic for 5 minutes. Stir in the flour and add the stock. Clean and trim the celery, then cut into small pieces and add to the pan. Season and simmer for 30–45 minutes or until celery is tender. Liquidise the soup, then return to the pan, adding the milk and nutmeg. Reheat the soup gently (do not boil) and adjust seasoning. Serve with croûtons.

QUICK SOUPS

These can be made with small packet soups (first checking for animal ingredients). I make up the soup, as per instructions, then add a selection of fresh vegetables, chopped into small pieces, together with ½ teaspoon yeast extract, some mixed cereals and pulses and whatever herbs or flavourings take the fancy. To packet mushroom soup, I add lots of slices of fresh mushrooms and a little milk for a filling starter to any meal.

STARTERS

MUSHROOM MELANGE
Cooking time about 25 minutes
SERVES 4

3–4 tablespoons olive oil
1 clove garlic, crushed
1 large onion, finely
  chopped
pinch thyme
1 bay leaf

450 g/1 lb button
  mushrooms
6 tomatoes, skinned
salt and pepper
chopped fresh parsley
triangles of thin wholewheat
  toast

Put the olive oil, garlic, onion, thyme and bay leaf into a pan. Bring to the boil and simmer for a few minutes.

Wipe the mushrooms and trim the stalks. Quarter and deseed the tomatoes and add to the oil mixture with the whole mushrooms. Season to taste. Bring to the boil and simmer with the pan lid on until the mushrooms are tender. Transfer them to a serving dish. Remove the bay leaf. Replace the lid and simmer the sauce mixture until it is reduced by about half. Pour over the mushrooms. Serve either hot or chilled with a sprinkling of fresh parsley on triangles of crisp thin wholewheat toast.

PEPPERS STUFFED WITH CHEESE
Cooking time 35 minutes
Oven temperature Moderate 180°C, 350°F Gas Mark 4
SERVES 4

4 medium green peppers
1 small onion
350 g/12 oz cottage cheese
3 sticks of celery, chopped

100 g/4 oz button
  mushrooms, chopped
salt and pepper
300 ml/½ pint tomato juice

Cut the peppers in half crossways and remove the stalks and seeds. Place them in a pan of boiling water and blanch for 5 minutes, then drain. Grate the onion and mix with the cottage cheese, celery, button mushrooms and salt and pepper. Spoon the mixture into the pepper halves and stand in a greased ovenproof dish. Pour the tomato juice around the peppers. Cover with foil and bake in a moderate oven for 30 minutes until tender.

ASPARAGUS TOPPER
Cooking time about 10 minutes
SERVES 4

4 slices wholemeal bread
25 g/1 oz butter or
  margarine
2 283-g/10-oz cans asparagus
  spears

175 g/6 oz Cheddar cheese
pinch cayenne pepper and
  chopped fresh parsley to
  garnish

Toast the wholemeal bread on both sides and spread one side with the butter or margarine. Drain the asparagus spears and arrange side by side on the toast. Slice the cheese and place over the asparagus. Put under a hot grill until the cheese melts and turns golden brown. Garnish with cayenne pepper and a sprinkling of chopped fresh parsley. Serve on a bed of seasoned shredded crisp lettuce.

EGGS IN ONION SAUCE
Cooking time 15 minutes
SERVES 4 or 8

8 hard-boiled eggs
4 medium onions
50 g/2 oz margarine or
  butter
25 g/1 oz flour

150 g/¼ pint milk
150 g/¼ pint double cream
salt and pepper
chopped chives to garnish

Keep the hard-boiled eggs (see page 145) warm until needed. Finely slice the onions and fry gently in the margarine or butter until soft but still white. Stir in the flour, gradually adding the milk and cream. Slowly bring to the boil, stirring, and simmer for a few minutes, adding salt and pepper to taste. Cut the hard-boiled eggs into quarters and arrange in a heated serving dish. Pour the onion sauce over and serve with a sprinkling of chopped chives.

HONEYDEW COCKTAIL
SERVES 4

1 honeydew melon
175 g/6 oz Cyprus sultana
  grapes, peeled

4 tablespoons crème de
  menthe
sprigs of mint to garnish

For each serving, fill a stemmed sundae glass with equal quantities of peeled, cubed honeydew melon and grapes. Pour 1 tablespoon crème de menthe over each serving. Chill well and garnish with small sprigs of fresh mint.

AVOCADO TANGY
SERVES 4

2 ripe avocado pears
1 85-g/3-oz packet cream
  cheese
1 small onion, finely grated

salt and black pepper
50 g/2 oz Cheddar cheese,
  grated

Halve the avocados and remove the stones. Carefully scoop out the flesh, leaving the 'shells' intact. Mix with the cream cheese and grated onion. Add seasoning to taste and pile back in the shells. Smooth over and sprinkle with the grated cheese.

HOT SPICED GRAPEFRUIT
Cooking time 8–10 minutes or 15 minutes
Oven temperature Moderately hot 200°C, 400°F, Gas Mark 6
SERVES 4

2 grapefruit
4 teaspoons molasses
ground cinnamon

a little soyanutta, peanut
butter or butter

Cut the grapefruit in half, remove the pips and cut between the segments. Dribble 1 teaspoon molasses over each grapefruit half and sprinkle each with a little ground cinnamon. Dot with a few flakes of soyanutta or butter. Place under a medium grill for 8–10 minutes until heated through, or place in an ovenproof dish in a moderately hot oven for about 15 minutes. A quick and easy dish to serve as the first course of a meal.

TOMATORANGE
SERVES 4

450 g/1 lb tomatoes, skinned
1 small orange, peeled
3 tablespoons salted peanuts
juice of 1 orange

3 tablespoons oil
2 tablespoons chopped fresh
parsley
black pepper

Slice the tomatoes thinly. Arrange in a shallow serving dish with thin slices of orange and salted peanuts. Mix the orange juice with the oil and chopped parsley, adding black pepper to taste. Spoon this dressing over the tomatoes and chill.

EGGS IN YOGURT
Cooking time 5 minutes
SERVES 4

2 cloves garlic
4 142-ml/5-fl oz cartons
natural yogurt
4 eggs

50 g/2 oz butter or
margarine
1 teaspoon paprika
salt and pepper

Crush the garlic with a little salt and mix with the yogurt. Pour the yogurt into 4 individual serving dishes. Cook the eggs in a poacher, then place a poached egg in the yogurt in each dish. Melt the butter or margarine, add the paprika and seasoning, then pour over the yogurt. Serve while the eggs are still hot.

MINTY CUCUMBER
SERVES 4

1 small cucumber
salt and pepper
4 spring onions, chopped
1 teaspoon caraway seeds

1 tablespoon fresh mint, chopped
150 g/¼ pint natural yogurt

Slice the cucumber thinly, sprinkle with salt and leave in a colander to drain. Rinse the cucumber and drain again. Mix with the spring onions, caraway seeds, mint, pepper and yogurt. Serve immediately.

EGG COCKTAIL
Cooking time 8 minutes
SERVES 6

6 eggs
1 teaspoon sultanas
1 teaspoon lemon juice
150 ml/¼ pint mayonnaise
2 teaspoons curry powder

2 teaspoons chutney
lettuce leaves
paprika
lemon twists to garnish

Hard-boil the eggs for 8 minutes. Cool under running cold water, then remove the shells. Cover the eggs with cold water until needed. Soak the sultanas in the lemon juice, then mix with the mayonnaise, curry powder and chutney (chop any large pieces). Dry the eggs thoroughly and chop them coarsely. Stir gently into the mayonnaise mixture.

Finely shred the lettuce and half fill 6 serving glasses. Spoon the egg mixture on top of the lettuce and sprinkle with paprika. Place the lemon twists on the side of each glass to serve.

GRAPEFRUIT CUPS
SERVES 4

2 grapefruits
1 green apple, cored and
  chopped
1 red apple, cored and
  chopped
2 sticks of celery, chopped

1 142-ml/5-fl oz carton
  natural yogurt
shredded lettuce leaves
¼ teaspoon nutmeg
slices of apple and cinnamon
  to garnish

Cut the grapefruit in half, scoop out the flesh (preferably using a grapefruit knife) and roughly chop. Mix the grape-fruit with the remaining ingredients. Fill each grapefruit half with the mixture and chill slightly. Garnish with an apple slice and a sprinkling of cinnamon.

CHEESE AND FRUIT COCKTAIL
SERVES 4

2 eating apples, chopped
1 tablespoon lemon juice
2 sticks celery, chopped
½ green pepper, chopped
4 oz Cheddar cheese, cubed

4 oz grapes, halved and de-
  seeded
shredded lettuce
1 orange
5 tablespoons cream

Put the apples in a bowl and sprinkle the lemon juice over. Add the celery, green pepper, cheese and grapes. Mix well. Put some shredded lettuce in the bases of 4 stemmed glass dishes and spoon the fruit and cheese mixture on top. Squeeze the juice from the orange and mix with some of the finely grated rind and cream. Pour some of the juice over each cocktail and serve chilled.

MUSHROOM AND CHEDDAR SCALLOPS

Cooking time 35 minutes
Oven temperature Moderate 180°C, 350°F Gas Mark 4

SERVES 4

1 medium onion, finely
  chopped
225 g/8 oz mushrooms
1 clove garlic, crushed
40 g/1½ oz butter
for the coating sauce
25 g/1 oz butter

25 g/1 oz flour
300 ml/½ pint milk
¼ teaspoon salt
pepper
25 g/1 oz Cheddar cheese,
  grated
1 tablespoon single cream

Fry the onion, thickly sliced mushrooms and garlic gently in
the butter. Divide the mixture equally between 4 clean scallop
shells or individual ovenproof dishes.

To make the coating sauce, melt the butter and stir in the
flour. Gradually add the milk, stirring all the time, until the
sauce thickens and bubbles. Add seasoning to taste. Remove
from the heat, add the grated cheese and cream, and pour
the sauce over the mushroom mixture. Sprinkle a little grated
Cheddar cheese over each serving. Bake in a moderate oven
for about 15 minutes. Serve hot with a green salad.

SUNNY COURGETTES

Cooking time about 20 minutes
Oven temperature Moderately hot 200°C, 400°F, Gas Mark 6

SERVES 4

4 medium size courgettes
1 150-g/5-oz carton plain
  yogurt
25 g/1 oz butter
1 carrot, grated
1 large onion, chopped
  finely

100 g/4 oz wholewheat
  breadcrumbs
100 g/4 oz sunflower seeds,
  lightly roasted and
  chopped
½ teaspoon basil
¼ teaspoon chilli powder
salt and black pepper

Cut the courgettes in half lengthways and scoop out the flesh.
Using only half the flesh, chop it finely and fry in the butter

along with the carrot, onion and breadcrumbs for about 10 minutes until lightly browned. Stir in the chilli powder, basil and sunflower seeds. Remove from heat, add yogurt and seasoning. Spoon into the courgette shells and bake in moderately hot oven for 10 minutes.

COURGETTE AND GARLIC PÂTÉ
Cooking time 25 minutes
SERVES 2

25g/1 oz butter
1 large onion, roughly chopped
2 cloves garlic, finely chopped

225 g/8 oz courgettes
100 g/4 oz cream cheese
4 tablespoons chopped fresh chives
salt and black pepper

Fry the onions and garlic gently in the butter in a large pan, shaking the pan from time to time to avoid sticking. Top and tail courgettes and cut into thin slices, then add to the pan and cook for a further 10–15 minutes until the courgettes are soft (but not too soft; ie retaining a little firmness).

When cooled, liquidise half the mixture with the cheese and chopped chives. Roughly chop the remaining mixture and stir into the liquidised pâté. Season, then chill.

Serve with crusty French bread, crispbread, French toast or any other similar crispy base.

This is a delicious and delicate pâté which makes a mouthwatering starter or snack.

Main Meals

Here are some ideas for main course meals which are filling and easy to make. I have included Textured Vegetable Protein (TVP) meals in this section.

WHOLEWHEAT CHEESE AND TOMATO PIE
Cooking time about 30 minutes
Oven temperature Moderately Hot 190°C, 375°F, Gas Mark 5
SERVES 4–6

225 g/8 oz shortcrust pastry (using 225 g/8 oz wholewheat flour and 75 g/3 oz margarine etc.)
225 g/8 oz Lancashire or Cheshire cheese, crumbled

3 large tomatoes, skinned and finely chopped
little milk
pepper

Line 20-cm/8-inch ovenproof plate with half the pastry. Mix the crumbled cheese and chopped tomatoes well and place over low heat for a few minutes. Stir in enough milk to mix to a fairly smooth consistency. Add the pepper, pile on to the pastry base and spread evenly. Cover with the pastry top and bake in a moderately hot oven for about 20 minutes.

CASHEW NUT ROAST
Cooking time 30 minutes
Oven temperature Hot 220°C, 425°F, Gas Mark 7
SERVES 4

225 g/8 oz cashew nuts, lightly roasted and finely grated
1 medium onion, finely chopped

225 g/8 oz tomatoes, skinned and finely chopped
2 eggs
1 teaspoon mixed herbs
pinch salt

Mix the cashew nuts, onion and the tomatoes together. Beat

61

the eggs and add to the mixture with the mixed herbs and salt. Spoon into a greased ovenproof dish and bake in a hot oven for 30 minutes. The roast will rise and is ready when it turns a golden brown colour. Serve with mashed potatoes, any green vegetables and vegetarian gravy (see below).

VEGETARIAN GRAVY
Cooking time 30 minutes
SERVES 6

1 medium onion, chopped
25 g/1 oz margarine or
   butter
4 tablespoons wholewheat
   flour
450 ml/¾ pint stock or
   water (or water from
   boiled greens)

1 bay leaf
2 tablespoons yeast extract
good pinch gravy salt
pepper
garlic salt (optional)

Once you've tasted this delicious recipe, you will not want to go back to 'ordinary' gravy.

Cook the onion gently in the margarine or butter until pale brown. Add the wholewheat flour and simmer for 5 minutes, stirring. Add the stock or water a little bit at a time and stir well. Add the bay leaf and simmer for 20 minutes.

If too thick, add a little more stock or water. Stir in the yeast extract and then the gravy salt, pepper and garlic salt. Remove the bay leaf and sieve the mixture.

TOAD IN THE HOLE
Cooking time about 30 minutes
Oven temperature Hot 220°C, 425°F, Gas Mark 7
SERVES 4

1 tablespoon oil
4 sausages, made from
   vegetarian sausage mix
for the batter
175 g/6 oz wholewheat flour

1 egg, beaten
milk
4 tablespoons water

Place the flour in a mixing bowl. Make a well in the centre and add the egg and enough milk and water to give a smooth batter. Beat thoroughly, adding more milk if required.

Heat a little oil in a 0.5-kg/1-lb loaf tin in a very hot oven until smoking. Put the sausages in the tin and pour the batter over. Reduce the heat and cook in a hot oven for 30 minutes until golden brown.

CAULIFLOWER ITALIENNE
Cooking time about 30 minutes
SERVES 4

1 medium cauliflower, trimmed	salt and black pepper
	25 g/1 oz breadcrumbs
25 g/1 oz butter	*for the sauce*
1 tablespoon oil	40 g/1½ oz margarine
1 medium onion, finely sliced	40 g/1½ oz flour
	150 ml/¼ pint water from cooking cauliflower
450 g/1 lb tomatoes	300 ml/½ pint milk
1 teaspoon chopped fresh parsley	100 g/4 oz cheese, grated

Divide the cauliflower in sprigs and cook in boiling salted water for 10 minutes. Pour off 150 ml/¼ pint water for making the sauce, then drain the cauliflower and keep warm. Meanwhile, melt the butter and oil into a saucepan, add the onion and cook for 5 minutes.

Plunge the tomatoes into boiling water for 10 seconds, then into cold water to make the skins shed easily. Remove any hard parts. Cut the tomatoes into quarters and add to the onion with the chopped parsley, salt and pepper. Cook gently together for a few minutes.

Make the sauce by melting the margarine in a pan. Remove from the heat and stir in the flour. Add the reserved cauliflower water and milk, then return to the heat, stir until smooth and bring to the boil. Stir in about 75 g/3 oz grated cheese and mix the remainder of the cheese with the bread-crumbs for the top. Season the sauce well. Put the tomato mixture over the base of a heated ovenproof dish and arrange the cooked cauliflower on top. Pour over the cheese sauce and finally sprinkle the cheese and breadcrumbs on. Place under a hot grill until the mixture is bubbling and golden brown.

Serve with new potatoes, if in season.

WHOLEWHEAT YORKSHIRE PUDDINGS
Cooking time 30 minutes
Oven temperature Very Hot 240°C, 475°, Gas Mark 9
MAKES ABOUT 12 PUDDINGS

175 g/6 oz wholewheat flour   water
1 egg   little oil
3 tablespoons milk

Place the flour in a mixing bowl and make a well in the centre. Pour in the egg and milk. Mix well and add enough water to make a smooth, but not too thick, batter.

Place a little oil in individual Yorkshire pudding or patty tins and put in a very hot oven until the oil is beginning to smoke. Pour in the batter and cook for 30 minutes until golden brown, turning after 15 minutes to cook the underside.

FARMERS SAUSAGEMEAT HOTPOT
Cooking time 1 hour
Oven temperature Moderate 180°C, 350°F, Gas Mark 4
SERVES 4

450 g/1 lb reconstituted vegetarian sausage mix
2 sticks of celery, finely chopped
1 small onion, finely chopped
1 396-g/14-oz can tomatoes
1 cooking apple, peeled, cored and sliced
1 teaspoon herbs
100 g/4 oz Cheddar cheese, grated
salt and pepper
900 g/2 lb mashed potatoes

Place the sausagemeat in an ovenproof dish. Mix the celery, onion, chopped tomatoes, apple, mixed herbs, 50 g/2 oz cheese, salt and pepper together and place on the sausage-meat. Top with the mashed potato and remaining cheese. Bake in a moderate oven for 1 hour.

COUNTRY PIE
Cooking time about 55 minutes
Oven temperature Hot 220°C, 425°F, Gas Mark 7
SERVES 4

for the filling
225 g/8 oz carrots
450 g/1 lb potatoes
2 medium onions, chopped
chopped fresh mint and
  parsley
225 g/8 oz peas
for the sauce
50 g/2 oz butter
40 g/1½ oz wholewheat
  flour
150 ml/¼ pint vegetable
  cooking water

150 ml/¼ pint milk
75 g/3 oz cheese, grated
for the pastry
225 g/8 oz wholewheat flour
pinch salt
pinch dry mustard
75 g/3 oz margarine
100 g/4 oz cheese, grated
3 tablespoons water
little milk

For the filling, slice the carrots and potatoes. Cook in boiling salted water, adding the onion, herbs and peas after 10 minutes. Drain most of the mixture, reserving 150 ml/¼ pint of the cooking liquid for the sauce, but leaving a slightly sloppy consistency.

For the sauce, blend the butter and wholewheat flour together. Add the reserved water from the vegetables then the milk, stirring well. Stir in the grated cheese and simmer for a few minutes.

For the pastry, mix the flour and seasonings together, then rub in the margarine and add the cheese. Stir in the water and mix to obtain a fairly firm dough, adding a little milk if necessary. Allow to stand for five minutes.

Put all the vegetables into a greased pie dish. Add salt and pepper to taste, then pour over the cheese sauce. Cover with the pastry and bake in a hot oven for 25 minutes.

PEASE PUDDING
Cooking time 3 hours
SERVES 3–4

450 g/1 lb yellow split peas
2 sage leaves
1 large onion, thinly sliced
salt and pepper

1 tablespoon plain flour
1 egg, beaten
margarine

Soak the peas for a few hours, then place in pan with the sage leaves, onion and seasoning. Cover with warm water and bring to the boil. Cook gently for about 2 hours until the peas are tender. Stir frequently, adding more water as necessary.

When the peas are soft, press them and the onion through a sieve or liquidise. Mix the flour to a paste with the beaten egg and stir into the peas. Add more seasoning, if required. Grease a basin with a little margarine, spread the mixture into it and cover with greaseproof paper. Steam for about 1 hour, then serve.

CELERY AND CARROT CASSEROLE
Cooking time 1 hour 5 minutes
Oven temperature Moderate 180°C, 350°F, Gas Mark 4
SERVES 4

350 g/12 oz carrots
4 large sticks of celery
25 g/1 oz butter
1 tablespoon tomato purée

300 ml/½ pint stock
bouquet garni
bay leaf
salt and pepper

Dice the carrots and chop the celery into small pieces. Melt the butter in a flameproof casserole and add the vegetables. Cover and cook gently for 5 minutes, then stir in the tomato purée and stock. Add the bouquet garni and bay leaf. Season and cook in a moderate oven for 1 hour.

ONION AND PARSLEY TART

Cooking time about 50 minutes
Oven temperature Moderately Hot 190°C, 375°F, Gas Mark 5

SERVES 4

225 g/8 oz shortcrust pastry
1 large onion, finely
  chopped
50 g/2 oz butter
2 tablespoons chopped fresh
  parsley

100 g/4 oz cheese, grated
3 eggs
150 ml/¼ pint milk
150 ml/¼ pint single cream
salt and pepper

Line a flan dish or shallow pie plate with the shortcrust pastry. Prick the base and bake blind for 10 minutes (see page 89). Fry the onion in the butter until soft and spoon into the pastry case. Sprinkle with the chopped parsley and grated cheese. Beat the eggs with the milk and cream, then season. Pour over the onion and parsley and bake in a moderately hot oven for 35–40 minutes until set.

MACARONI CHEESE BURGERS

Cooking time 30 minutes

SERVES 4

175 g/6 oz short cut
  macaroni
75 g/3 oz margarine
75 g/3 oz flour
450 ml/¾ pint milk
175 g/6 oz cheese, grated

salt and pepper
pinch dry mustard
2 hard-boiled eggs, chopped
for the coating
2 eggs, beaten
breadcrumbs

Cook the macaroni for 10 minutes in boiling salted water, then drain and rinse under cold running water until cold. To make the thick cheese sauce, melt the margarine, add the flour and cook for 1 minute. Gradually add the milk, stirring all the time. Remove from heat and add the cheese, seasoning, and pinch mustard. Add the macaroni and chopped eggs and leave to cool. When cool and firm, shape into round flat burgers, coat with the beaten egg and breadcrumbs. Shallow or deep fry for about 10 minutes until golden, then serve.

WHOLEWHEAT PASTA WITH GORGONZOLA SAUCE
Cooking time 20 minutes
SERVES 4

350 g/12 oz wholewheat
  pasta
50 g/2 oz Gorgonzola cheese
100 g/4 oz cottage cheese
1 clove garlic, peeled
4–6 tablespoons single cream
salt and pepper

50 g/2 oz butter
½ green pepper, finely
  chopped
4 spring onions, finely
  chopped

Boil the pasta in plenty of boiling salted water, for about 10 minutes. Meanwhile, prepare the sauce by putting the cheeses into a liquidiser, together with the garlic clove, cream and seasoning. Blend until smooth.

Thoroughly drain the pasta and quickly return it to a hot dry pan together with the butter, chopped pepper and spring onions. Season and toss well. Spoon the sauce over, toss again, allow to heat through and serve immediately on hot plates.

TANGY MEATBALLS
Cooking time 45 minutes
Oven temperature Moderately Hot 190°C, 375°F, Gas Mark 5
SERVES 4

350 g/12 oz reconstituted
  TVP mince
40 g/1½ oz breadcrumbs
1 large onion, finely
  chopped
salt and pepper
1 egg, beaten
flour
1 tablespoon oil
15 g/½ oz butter

1 298-g/10½-oz can
  condensed mushroom
  soup
150 ml/¼ pint milk
1 tablespoon chutney
1 tablespoon tomato sauce
1 tablespoon vinegar
chopped fresh parsley to
  garnish

Put the TVP mince, breadcrumbs, onion and seasoning into

a bowl and bind with the beaten egg. Shape into eight balls and coat with a little flour.

Heat the oil and butter in a frying pan and fry the meatballs until golden brown. Drain well and place in casserole dish. Blend the soup, milk, chutney, tomato sauce and vinegar, then pour over the meatballs. Bake in a moderately hot oven for 30 minutes. Serve on a bed of rice or noodles and sprinkle with chopped parsley.

EGG PIZZAS
Cooking time about 10 minutes
Oven temperature Hot 220°C, 425°F, Gas Mark 7
MAKES 6 PIZZAS

for the base
225 g/8 oz self-raising flour
75 g/3 oz soft butter or
  margarine
½ teaspoon salt
pepper
2 eggs
for the topping
3 tablespoons tomato purée
1 small onion, finely grated
¼ teaspoon oregano or
  marjoram
salt and pepper
6 hard-boiled eggs
15 black olives, stoned and
  halved
3 eggs, beaten
350 g/12 oz cheese, grated
1½ teaspoons made
  mustard

Put all the base ingredients in a bowl and gradually work together with a knife to make a firm dough. Roll out and cut six 10–13-cm/4–5-inch rounds and put them on a baking tray.

Mix the tomato purée with the onion, oregano and seasoning. Spread over each dough base to the edges. Cut the hard-boiled eggs in half, then put two, flat side down, in the middle of each base. Arrange the olives around the edge. Mix the eggs, cheese, mustard and seasoning, then spoon the mixture over the pizza bases. Bake in a hot oven for about 10 minutes until bubbling and golden brown on top.

If required, make one large pizza and bake for about 20 minutes.

Note: These pizzas are ideal picnic food, served with salad.

Wrap each cold pizza separately and pack into a tin or polythene container to carry.

MACARONI EGGS
Cooking time 35 minutes
Oven temperature Moderately Hot 200°C, 400°F, Gas Mark 6
SERVES 4

40 g/1½ oz macaroni	salt and pepper
20 g/¾ oz plain flour	little made mustard
300 ml/½ pint milk	40 g/1½ oz cheese, grated
40 g/1½ oz butter	8 eggs

Cook the macaroni in boiling salted water for about 15 minutes until just tender. Drain. Whisk the flour into the milk and add 15 g (½ oz) of the butter. Stir over a low heat until thickened and cooked. Add salt and pepper to taste, mustard and cheese.

Butter 4 individual dishes, mix the macaroni with half the sauce and spoon into the dishes. Break 2 eggs into each dish, cover with the remaining sauce and bake in a moderately hot oven for about 10 minutes. Serve hot with green vegetables.

ANDALUSIAN EGGS
Cooking time about 30 minutes
Oven temperature Moderately Hot 200°C, 400°F, Gas Mark 6
SERVES 4

3 tablespoons oil	1 425-g/15-oz can or 350 g/
1 large onion, finely	12 oz tomatoes
chopped	salt and pepper
1 clove garlic, finely	8 eggs
chopped	
2 red peppers	

Heat the oil in a flameproof dish and fry the onion and garlic gently for 5 minutes. Remove the stalks and seeds from the peppers, then chop finely and add to the dish. Cook for a further 5 minutes. Skin and slice the tomatoes, add to the dish with the seasoning and heat through. Break the eggs on top and spoon juices over the eggs. Bake in a moderately hot oven for up to 10 minutes. Serve hot with bread and a green salad.

CHEESE PUDDING
Cooking time 45 minutes
Oven temperature Moderately Hot 190°C, 375°F, Gas Mark 5
SERVES 4

300 ml/½ pint milk	¼ teaspoon salt
15 g/½ oz butter	pepper
350 g/12 oz fresh breadcrumbs	¼ teaspoon made mustard
	¼ teaspoon yeast extract
50 g/2 oz cheese, grated	1 egg, separated

Heat the milk and butter, add the breadcrumbs and cook gently for a few minutes. Remove from the heat, add the cheese. seasonings, yeast extract and yolk of the egg. Beat the white very stifly and fold lightly into the mixture. Pour into a greased ovenproof dish and bake in a moderately hot oven for about 40 minutes until well risen and brown.

POTATO AND CHEESE SOUFFLÉ
Cooking time 50 minutes
Oven temperature Moderately Hot 200°C. 400°F, Gas Mark 6
SERVES 4

675 g/1½ lb potatoes	2 tablespoons cream or top of the milk
100 g/4 oz cheese, grated	
3 eggs, separated	salt
25 g/1 oz butter	pinch cayenne pepper

Thinly peel the potatoes and boil in salted water. When cooked, drain well and press through a sieve. Beat the sieved potato with the cheese, egg yolks, butter and cream until smooth. Season with salt and cayenne pepper. Whisk the egg whites until stiff and fold very lightly into the mixture. Pour into a greased soufflé dish and bake in a moderately hot oven for about 30 minutes. Serve with a crisp green salad.

SAVOYARDE EGGS
Cooking time about 1 hour 45 minutes
Oven temperature Moderately Hot 190°C, 375°F, Gas Mark 5
SERVES 4

675 g/1½ lb potatoes
350 g/12 oz onions
50 g/2 oz butter
salt and pepper
8 eggs

150 ml/¼ pint single cream
  or milk
50 g/2 oz cheese, grated
chopped fresh parsley to
  garnish

Slice potatoes and onions thickly. Butter a shallow casserole dish and fill with layers of potato and onion, adding pieces of butter and seasoning to each layer. Cover with the lid or foil and bake in a moderately hot oven for about 1½ hours.

Poach the eggs and arrange on top of the potato mixture. Pour the cream over, sprinkle with cheese and place under a heated grill to melt and brown the cheese. Garnish with chopped parsley.

RATATOUILLE
Cooking time 1 hour
SERVES 4

2 large aubergines
salt and pepper
6 tablespoons olive oil
2 onions, sliced
2 red or green peppers

450 g/1 lb courgettes, sliced
2 cloves garlic, crushed,
450 g/1 lb tomatoes, skinned
  and chopped
½ teaspoon dried basil

Dice the aubergines into about 1-cm/½-inch pieces. Place in a colander and sprinkle with salt. Leave to drain for 1 hour, then rinse and drain again. Heat the oil and fry the onions until soft. Cut the peppers into strips and add to the onions with the courgette, aubergine and garlic.

Cover and simmer for about 30 minutes. Add the tomatoes, basil and seasoning. Continue cooking over a low heat for about 15–20 minutes, until the vegetables are soft and any excess liquid has evaporated.

BAKED BEAN LASAGNE
Cooking time 1 hour 10 minutes
Oven temperature Moderately Hot 200°C, 400°F, Gas Mark 6
SERVES 6–8

225 g/8 oz wholewheat
  lasagne
450 g/1 lb onions, chopped
1 tablespoon oil
100 g/14 oz mushrooms,
  sliced

1 447-g/15¾-oz can baked
  beans
2 tablespoons tomato
  ketchup
900 ml/1½ pints cheese
  sauce
25 g/1 oz cheese, grated

Cook the lasagne in boiling salted water, as directed on the packet. Fry the onions in the oil until soft but not brown, then add the mushrooms and cook for a further minute. Add the baked beans and tomato ketchup and mix well.

Meanwhile, make up the cheese sauce. Place a layer of lasagne in the bottom of a greased ovenproof dish, cover with half the baked beans mixture and a little of the cheese sauce. Repeat these layers, finishing with the lasagne. Top with the remaining cheese sauce and the grated cheese. Bake in a moderately hot oven for 40 minutes.

ONION AND PARSNIP LOAF
Cooking time about 1 hour 10 minutes
Oven temperature Moderate 180°C, 350°F, Gas Mark 4
SERVES 4

450 g/1 lb parsnips, cooked
1 large onion, chopped
25 g/1 oz butter
chopped fresh parsley
1½ tablespoons chopped
  fresh thyme

2 eggs, beaten
salt and pepper
chopped fresh chives or
  parsley to garnish

Mash the cooked parsnips. Fry the onion in the butter until starting to brown. Mix together the onion, parsnip, parsley, thyme, eggs, salt and pepper, and place in a greased loaf tin. Cover with foil and bake in a moderate oven for 1 hour.

Eat hot or cold garnished with chopped chives or parsley, and serve with a side salad.

LEEK AND MUSHROOM TASTY
Cooking time 55 minutes
Oven temperature Moderate 180°C, 350°F, Gas Mark 4
SERVES 4

225 g/8 oz leeks
175 g/6 oz noodles or
spaghetti rings
175 ml/½ pint water
175 g/6 oz mushrooms,
chopped

salt and pepper
pinch mixed herbs
pinch garlic salt
600 ml/1 pint cheese sauce
50 g/2 oz cheese, grated

Wash the leeks thoroughly, removing the green outer leaves. Slice into rings and cover the base of a casserole dish with half of them. Spoon over half the uncooked pasta and pour on the water. Fry the mushrooms lightly in another pan and add the seasonings. Add half the mushrooms to the casserole. Repeat the layers with the remaining leeks, pasta and mushrooms. Cover with the cheese sauce and sprinkle the grated cheese over the top. Bake in a moderate oven for 45 minutes.

POTATO HASH SCRAMBLE
Cooking time about 15 minutes
SERVES 3–4

25 g/1 oz butter
450 g/1 lb mashed potatoes
for the filling
1 small onion, finely
chopped

2 tomatoes, sliced
25 g/1 oz butter
2–3 eggs
salt and pepper

Heat the butter in a frying pan and add the mashed potato, pressing down with a knife. Allow to cook gently until the underneath is brown and crisp.

Meanwhile. sauté the onion and tomato in the butter in a

74

small saucepan, add the lightly beaten eggs and seasoning, and scramble until creamy. Spoon the scrambled egg mixture on to the potato, fold over carefully and slide on to a hot serving plate.

UPSIDE-DOWN POTATO
Cooking time 45 minutes
Oven temperature Moderately Hot 190°C, 375°F, Gas Mark 5
SERVES 4

225 g/8 oz cooked potatoes, diced	225 g/8 oz self-raising flour
	75 g/3 oz butter
225 g/8 oz mixed vegetables, cooked	1 egg, beaten
	milk to mix
1 227-g/8-oz can tomatoes	75 g/3 oz Cheddar cheese,
salt and pepper	grated

Place the potatoes and vegetables in a round greased oven-proof dish, pour the tomatoes over and season.

Sift the flour into a mixing bowl, add a little salt and rub in the butter until it resembles fine breadcrumbs. Add the beaten egg and enough milk to make a soft dough. Roll out the dough to the size of the dish and place over the vegetables. Brush with a little egg or milk and bake in a moderately hot oven for 30–35 minutes. When cooked, turn out on to an ovenproof serving dish. Sprinkle with the cheese and return to the oven for a further 10 minutes to melt the cheese.

FAMILY FAVOURITE CASSEROLE
Cooking time 1 hour 30 minutes
Oven temperature Moderate 180°C, 350°F, Gas Mark 4
SERVES 4

450 g/1 lb potatoes
2 tablespoons oil
225 g/8 oz marrow or
    aubergine, peeled and
    sliced

225 g/8 oz tomatoes, sliced
225 g/8 oz onions, sliced
salt and pepper
225 g/8 oz cheese, grated

Peel the potatoes very thinly and parboil in salted water for 5–10 minutes, depending upon the size. Drain and cut into thick slices, about 2 cm/¾ inch thick. Heat the oil in a frying pan and sauté the marrow or aubergine, tomato and onion, but do not brown. Arrange layers of all the vegetables with seasoning in a greased-baking dish, finishing with a layer of potato. Sprinkle with the cheese and bake in a moderately hot oven for 1–1¼ hours.

If the top is not sufficiently browned, just place under a heated grill for a few seconds.

POTATO AND LENTIL GOULASH
Cooking time about 40 minutes
Oven temperature Moderately Hot 190°C, 375°F, Gas Mark 5
SERVES 4

450 g/1 lb potatoes, boiled
1 large onion, chopped
25 g/1 oz butter
2 tablespoons tomato purée
1 396 g/14 oz can tomatoes
2 tablespoons
    Worcestershire sauce

1 142 ml/5-fl oz carton
    soured cream
75 g/3 oz lentils, soaked
50 g/2 oz cheese, grated

Thickly slice the potatoes. Lightly fry the onion in the butter, then add the tomato purée, canned tomatoes and Worcestershire sauce. Stir in the soured cream.

Line the bottom of a greased ovenproof dish with potato slices, then arrange alternate layers of lentils and potatoes.

Pour the tomato mixture over and sprinkle with the cheese. Bake in a moderately hot oven for about 30 minutes until the cheese is browned.

STUFFED ONIONS
Cooking time 45 minutes
Oven temperature Moderate 180°C, 350°F, Gas Mark 4
SERVES 4

4 large onions
50 g/2 oz cheese, grated
1 tablespoon grated cashew
  nuts

2 tablespoons fine dry
  breadcrumbs
40 g/1½ oz butter
salt and pepper

Boil the peeled whole onions in slightly salted water until tender, but still retaining their round shape. Remove the onions from the water, drain and cool. Remove the centres carefully, chop finely and mix with the cheese, nuts, breadcrumbs, 25 g/1 oz of the butter, melted. Add seasoning to taste.

Fill each onion with the mixture. Using the remaining butter, well grease a baking tray. Place the stuffed onions on the tray and bake in a moderate oven until the onions are browned.

CURRIED LENTILS
Cooking time about 1 hour 10 minutes
SERVES 4

50 g/2 oz lentils
1 small onion, chopped
1½ teaspoons curry powder
15 g/½ oz margarine
1 tablespoon chopped apple
½ teaspoon salt

pepper
1 teaspoon lemon juice or
  chutney
150 ml/¼ pint water
½ teaspoon yeast extract

Wash and soak the lentils for several hours. Fry the onion, sprinkled with the curry powder in the margarine. Add the lentils, apple, salt, pepper, lemon juice or chutney. Simmer for about 1 hour until the lentils are tender, adding more water if required. Stir in the yeast extract and serve with boiled rice.

FARMER'S FILL
Cooking time about 50 minutes
Oven temperature Moderate 180°C, 350°F, Gas Mark 4
SERVES 4

50 g/2 oz butter	good pinch garlic salt
225 g/8 oz lentils, soaked	pepper
225 g/8 oz turnips, diced	225 g/8 oz swede
225 g/8 oz onions, sliced	450 g/1 lb potatoes
225 g/8 oz parsnips, diced	

Put half the butter in a pan and simmer the lentils, turnips, onions and parsnips with just enough water to stop the vegetables sticking — adding more water, if necessary. When the vegetables and lentils are tender, season and place in a 1.5-litre/2½-pint ovenproof dish.

Meanwhile, cut the swede and potatoes in pieces and boil together. When cooked, season and mash together with the remaining butter. Spread over the lentil mixture and make a criss-cross pattern on the top with a knife. Bake in a moderate oven for about 20–30 minutes until crisp and browned.

This is a cheap dish and very filling, too.

KING LEEK LIPSMACKER
Cooking time about 1 hour
Oven temperature Moderately Hot 200°C, 400°F, Gas Mark 6
SERVES 4–5

675 g/1½ lb potatoes	25 g/1 oz plain flour
6 leeks	300 ml/½ pint milk
knob of butter	75 g/3 oz Cheddar cheese
8 hard-boiled eggs	
for the sauce	
25 g/1 oz butter	

Boil the potatoes in salted water, drain and mash. Cut the leeks into rings and cook in salted water for 10 minutes. Drain well. Add the leeks to the potatoes with the knob of butter and beat well to give a fluffy pale green mixture.

Make up the cheese sauce (see page 63), using 60 g/2½ oz of the cheese. Spoon the leek and potato mixture into an ovenproof dish and fork over the top. Cut the eggs in half, arrange in the dish and coat with the cheese sauce. Sprinkle the remaining grated cheese on top and bake in a moderately hot oven for about 20 minutes until the top is golden.

SAVOURY ROAST
Cooking time 45 minutes
Oven temperature Moderate 180°C, 350°F, Gas Mark 4
SERVES 4

225 g/8 oz savoury powder
   (such as Savormix or
   Frittamix)
450 g/1 lb onions
4 tablespoons strong
   vegetable stock

salt and pepper
450 g/1 lb mashed potatoes
25 g/1 oz butter or
   margarine

Add enough water to the savoury powder to make a wet paste. Mince the onions. Add the vegetable stock to the minced onions, season to taste and spoon alternate layers of onions and savoury paste into a greased pie dish. Cover with the mashed potato and knobs of butter or margarine. Bake in a moderate oven for 45 minutes. Serve with vegetables and vegetarian gravy (see page 62).

VEGETABLE RISSOLES
Cooking time about 1 hour 50 minutes
Oven temperature Moderately Hot 190°C, 375°F, Gas Mark 5
SERVES 4

50 g/2 oz haricot beans
50 g/2 oz dried green peas
½ beaten egg
15 g/½ oz butter or
   margarine
salt and pepper
1 small onion, partly cooked
½ teaspoon chopped fresh
   parsley

½ teaspoon dried or fresh
   mixed herbs
½ teaspoon yeast extract
for the coating
beaten egg
dried breadcrumbs

Soak the haricot beans and peas. Cook them together in slightly salted water for about 1½ hours. Drain and press through a sieve. Cook the egg in the melted butter or margarine, then stir in the seasoning, onion, parsley, mixed herbs, yeast extract and pea and bean purée. Turn on to a plate to cool.

Divide the mixture and form into cakes, cutlets or rissoles. Coat with the beaten egg and breadcrumbs and deep fry in hot oil until golden brown. Alternatively, bake in a moderately hot oven in a greased casserole with browned breadcrumbs and pats of butter on top. Serve with a tomato or onion sauce, boiled potatoes and green vegetables.

EGGS AU GRATIN SOUBISE
Cooking time about 55 minutes
Oven temperature Moderate 180°C, 350°F, Gas Mark 4
SERVES 4

450 g/1 lb onions, sliced
40 g/1½ oz butter
100 g/4 oz Cheddar cheese,
   grated
50 g/2 oz breadcrumbs
salt and pepper

4 hard-boiled eggs, halved
for the pouring sauce
15 g/½ oz butter
15 g/½ oz flour
300 ml/½ pint milk
pinch marjoram

Boil the onion slices in salted water for 5 minutes, drain well and chop finely. Melt 25 g/1 oz butter in a pan and cook the onions gently until golden.

Mix the cheese and breadcrumbs and put half in the bottom of a buttered shallow ovenproof dish. Cover with half the onions and season with salt and pepper, with a pinch of garlic salt, if liked. Arrange the halved eggs on top.

For the sauce, melt the butter, add the flour and seasoning, and stir until smooth. Place over a low heat for a few minutes, stirring, until the mixture starts to bubble. Remove from the heat and gradually add the milk, stirring to prevent lumps forming. Bring to the boil, stirring continuously, and cook for 5 minutes. Add the marjoram and then pour the sauce over the eggs. Cover with the remaining onion and bread-crumb mixture. Dot with the remaining butter and bake in a moderate oven for 25 minutes. Alternatively, place under a heated grill until golden brown.

APPLE, POTATO AND SAUSAGE PIE
Cooking time 40–45 minutes
Oven temperature Moderately Hot 200°C, 400°F, Gas Mark 6
SERVES 2–3

225 g/8 oz cooking apples, peeled and sliced
25 g/1 oz sugar
1 medium onion, finely chopped

225 g/8 oz vegetarian sausage mix (e.g. Sosmix), reconstituted
225 g/8 oz mashed potatoes
2 tomatoes, sliced

Grease the base of a casserole dish, put the apple slices on the bottom and sprinkle with sugar. Mix the onion with the reconstituted sausagemeat and spoon over the apples. Spread the mashed potatoes over the mixture with a fork, then place the tomatoes on top. Bake in a moderately hot oven for 40–45 minutes.

SAUSAGE CARTWHEELS
Cooking time about 35 minutes
Oven temperature Moderate 180°C, 350°F, Gas Mark 4
SERVES 3–4

450 g/1 lb potatoes, cooked
  and sliced
1 medium onion, finely
  chopped
25 g/1 oz butter or
  margarine

225 g/8 oz reconstituted
  vegetarian sausage mix
½ tomato
2 eggs
150 ml/¼ pint milk

Put the potato slices in a round casserole dish. Fry the onion
lightly in the butter or margarine. Scatter the onion over the
potatoes. Shape the sausage mix into sausage shapes and
arrange them on top of the potato slices to look like the
spokes of a wheel. Place the tomato, cut side down, in the
centre of the dish. Beat the eggs and milk and pour into the
dish. Cook in a moderate oven for about 30 minutes until
the egg is set.

FLORENTINE PASTA
Cooking time about 40 minutes
Oven temperature Moderately Hot 200°C, 400°F, Gas Mark 6
SERVES 4

225 g/8 oz long macaroni
450 g/1 lb spinach

4 eggs
100 g/4 oz cheese, grated

Cook the pasta (see page 70), then drain. Place in the bottom
of a greased ovenproof serving dish. Meanwhile, cook the
spinach in very little water. Chop and arrange in a ring round
the edge of the dish. Beat the eggs and cheese and pour into
the centre of the spinach. Bake in a moderately hot oven for
10 minutes.

LENTIL AND NUT ROAST
Cooking time about 1 hour 40 minutes
Oven temperature Moderate 180°C, 350°F, Gas Mark 4
SERVES 4

¼ teaspoon salt
½ teaspoon yeast extract
600 ml/1 pint water or stock
100 g/4 oz lentils
75 g/3 oz milled or grated
  cashew nuts

100 g/4 oz breadcrumbs
1 teaspoon salt
pepper
1 egg, beaten
browned breadcrumbs to
  coat

Add the salt and yeast extract to the water or stock. Cook
the lentils in the stock until tender. Add the nuts and breadcrumbs and mix well. Season and add the beaten egg. Turn
the mixture into a tin, previously greased and coated with
the browned breadcrumbs. Bake in a moderate oven for
30–40 minutes. Serve with vegetarian gravy (see page 62) or
a savoury sauce.

EGG FARM SCRAMBLE
Cooking time 12 minutes
SERVES 4

450 g/1 lb green cabbage,
  shredded
8 eggs
salt and pepper

15 g/½ oz butter
2 tablespoons milk
2 tablespoons chopped
  capers

Cook the cabbage in boiling salted water for about 8 minutes
until just soft. Beat the eggs and add the salt and pepper.
Rub the butter round the inside of a wide saucepan then pour
in the eggs. Stir over a low heat until beginning to scramble.
Mix in the milk and continue stirring until just scrambled,
then add the capers.

Drain the cabbage and place in the bottom of a heated
serving dish. Pile the eggs on top and serve.

QUICK MINCE MIX
Cooking time 10 minutes
SERVES 2

6 tablespoons dry TVP
  mince, beef flavour if
  liked
150 ml/¼ pint water
1 small onion, finely
  chopped

1 teaspoon yeast extract
pinch garlic salt
pepper

Cook the mince in the water, with the chopped onion and yeast extract added, over a low heat for 10 minutes. Add the garlic salt and pepper. Serve with potatoes, green vegetables and vegetarian gravy (see page 62).

POTATO SCALLOPS
Cooking time about 40 minutes
SERVES 4

225 g/8 oz carrots
450 g/1 lb onions
1 tablespoon oil
1 kg/2 lb potatoes, sliced

50 g/2 oz lentils, soaked
little gravy salt
salt and pepper

Slice the carrots and onions thinly. Fry in the oil in a deep frying pan until the onions are transparent, about 10 minutes. Add the sliced potatoes and lentils and cook over a medium heat for 30 minutes, adding a little water from time to time, if necessary. Stir in the gravy salt and salt and pepper. Serve with dumplings (see page 109).

GNOCCHI ALLA ROMANA
Cooking time 50 minutes
Oven temperature Moderately Hot 190°C, 375°F, Gas Mark 5

SERVES 4

600 ml/1 pint milk
100 g/4 oz semolina
25 g/1 oz butter
1 egg, beaten
salt and pepper
50 g/2 oz grated Parmesan
3 hard-boiled eggs

for the sauce
40 g/1½ oz butter
40 g/1½ oz flour
450 ml/¾ pint milk
salt and pepper
½ teaspoon made mustard
50 g/2 oz grated Parmesan

Bring the milk to the boil, sprinkle in the semolina gradually.
Lower the heat and simmer for 10 minutes, stirring all the
time, until the mixture thickens. Add the butter, beaten eggs,
seasoning and Parmesan. Simmer for a few minutes until the
mixture is firm. Turn out on to a flat plate and, when cool,
divide in half. Shape each half into a cylinder. Slice into
rounds and place these in layers in a greased ovenproof dish
with the sliced hard-boiled eggs.

To make the sauce, melt the butter and add the flour,
stirring. Remove from the heat and gradually pour in the
milk. Return to the heat, stirring continuously until the sauce
bubbles. Add the seasoning, mustard, half the Parmesan and
spoon over the gnocchi. Sprinkle the remaining cheese over
the top. Bake in a moderate oven for about 30 minutes until
brown.

MILAN RISOTTO
Cooking time about 30 minutes

SERVES 4

175 g/6 oz long-grain rice
1 medium onion, finely
   chopped
25 g/1 oz butter
2 tomatoes

2 egg yolks
40 g/1½ oz Parmesan
salt and pepper
little vegetarian gravy (see
   page 62)

Cook the rice in boiling salt water for about 15 minutes.

Rinse and drain. Fry the onion in the butter. Boil the tomatoes until soft, then skin and mash with the egg yolks, Parmesan and seasoning. Add to the rice with the onion. Stir well and place over a low heat for about 15 minutes, adding enough gravy to keep the risotto moist. Serve hot.

CHEESE 'N' ONION PIE
Cooking time 45 minutes
Oven temperature Moderate 190°C, 375°F, Gas Mark 5
SERVES 4

225 g/8 oz shortcrust pastry little milk
2 medium onions pepper
225 g/8 oz Lancashire cheese,
 grated

Roll out half the pastry to a 5-mm/¼-inch thick circle, and use to line a 20-cm/8-inch ovenproof plate or pie dish.

Boil the onions for 20 minutes until soft. Drain and chop. Mix in the grated cheese with a little milk and simmer until the cheese melts. Stir well and add pepper to taste. Spoon into the centre of the pastry base and spread evenly. Cover with the other half of the pastry and seal the edges with a fork. Make two small slits in the centre of the pie with a knife and bake in a moderately hot oven for 25 minutes.

RICE AND TOMATO BAKE
Cooking time about 1 hour
Oven temperature Moderate 180°C, 350°F, Gas Mark 4
SERVES 4

225 g/8 oz rice
1½ teaspoons yeast extract
2 medium onions, finely
 chopped
25 g/1 oz margarine
1 396-g/14-oz can tomatoes
good pinch thyme

1 clove garlic, finely
 chopped, or good pinch
 garlic salt
1 teaspoon made mustard
salt and black pepper
225 g/8 oz Lancashire cheese
chopped fresh parsley

Boil the rice in slightly salted water with the yeast extract added. Meanwhile, fry the onions in the margarine for 10 minutes. Pouring off a little of the tomato juice, add the tomatoes to the onion. Break the tomatoes into the onions with a fork until the mixture is mushy. Add the thyme, garlic or garlic salt, mustard and a little salt and pepper. Simmer together vigorously, with the lid on, for 15–20 minutes.

Pour the tomato mixture into a casserole dish, then place the drained rice in a ring round the top. Crumble the cheese over the dish and bake in a moderate oven for about 20 minutes or until the cheese has melted and is beginning to brown. Sprinkle with chopped parsley and serve with sweet-corn niblets.

EGG AND VEGETABLE QUICKIE
Cooking time about 25 minutes
Oven temperature Moderate 180°C, 350°F, Gas Mark 4
SERVES 4

25 g/1 oz butter	4 hard-boiled eggs
25 g/1 oz flour	salt and pepper
1 teaspoon curry powder	1 small packet crisps
300 ml/½ pint milk	100 g/4 oz crumbly cheese,
1 340-g/12-oz packet frozen	such as Lancashire
mixed vegetables, cooked	

Melt the butter and stir in the flour and curry powder. Cook for about 1 minute, stirring. Gradually pour in the milk, stirring to make sure there are no lumps. Slowly bring to the boil and simmer for a couple of minutes before adding the cooked mixed vegetables.

Cut the eggs in half and place cut side down in an oven-proof dish. Pour the vegetable mixture over them and add salt and pepper. Sprinkle the crisps over the dish, then the crumbled cheese. Bake in a moderate oven for about 15 minutes or until the cheese begins to melt into the mixture.

SPAGHETTI IN TOMATO SAUCE

Cooking time 25 minutes

SERVES 4

for the sauce
1 large onion
4 tablespoons oil
1 clove garlic, chopped
675 g/1½ lb ripe tomatoes,
    skinned (or 2 400 g/14 oz
    cans of peeled canned
    tomatoes, chopped finely
    – plus the juice)
pinch thyme
½ teaspoon basil

¼ teaspoon oregano
1 tablespoon fresh parsley,
    finely chopped
salt and black pepper
2 teaspoons salt
225 g/8 oz spaghetti (best
    durum wheat or
    wholewheat)
15 g/½ oz butter
225 g/8 oz Cheddar cheese,
    grated

For the sauce, chop the onion finely and fry gently in the oil with the garlic for a few minutes. Add the tomatoes, halved and deseeded, herbs, salt and pepper. Bring to the boil, then simmer with the lid on, stirring occasionally, until the tomatoes are soft and the sauce cooked.

Meanwhile, boil 1.75–2.25 litres/3–4 pints water with the salt added. Carefully feed the spaghetti into the pan, until it curls round and is immersed in the water. Cook for about 10–15 minutes until the spaghetti is 'al dente', ie neither too hard nor too soft. Drain in a colander and place under running cold water. Melt the butter in the pan, return the spaghetti and shake until hot. Season with black pepper. Serve with the sauce and grated cheese.

Note: This recipe is also delicious with pasta shells or pasta spirals.

SPAGHETTI BOLOGNESE

Proceed as above, but when adding tomatoes and juice add 100 g/4 oz (reconstituted weight) TVP mince and stir well in. Add a dash of red wine if wished.

TOMATO QUICHE
Cooking time 1 hour
Oven temperatures Moderately Hot 190°C, 375°F, Gas Mark 5 then
Moderate 180°C, 350°F, Gas Mark 4
SERVES 4

225 g/8 oz shortcrust pastry
450 g/1 lb tomatoes, skinned
  and deseeded
1 small onion, chopped
1 teaspoon fresh parsley,
  chopped
1 teaspoon fresh basil,
  chopped

1 teaspoon fresh thyme,
  chopped
salt and pepper
1 egg
200 ml/7 fl oz milk
tomato slices and chopped
fresh parsley to garnish

Roll out the pastry and use to line a 20-cm/8-inch flan dish. Place a circle of greaseproof paper on to the pastry and fill with dried peas, beans or similar. Bake blind in a moderately hot oven for about 15 minutes. Remove the paper and bake for a further 10 minutes.

Meanwhile, slice the tomatoes thinly. Place in a saucepan with 2 tablespoons water, onion, herbs, salt and pepper. Bring to the boil and simmer until the tomatoes are cooked. Beat the egg and add the milk, then stir into the tomato mixture. Pour this mixture into the pastry case and bake in a moderate oven for about 35 minutes. Garnish with slices of tomato and chopped parsley. Serve with jacket potatoes and a crisp fresh salad.

CHEESY MILLET
Cooking time about 40 minutes
SERVES 4

175g/6 oz millet
1½ tablespoons oil
300 ml/½ pint vegetable
  stock or water

salt and pepper
25 g/1 oz butter
225 g/8 oz Cheddar cheese,
  grated

Brown the millet in the oil in a frying pan for 5–10 minutes. Place in a saucepan and add the stock or water, salt and pepper. Bring to boil and simmer gently for about 20–30 minutes, adding water if necessary. When swelled and cooked, stir in the butter, a drop of water and 175 g/6 oz of the cheese. Keep stirring over a low heat until the cheese melts into the millet. Sprinkle with the rest of the cheese and serve with a green vegetable, such as Brussels sprouts or broccoli.

SING-AS-WE-GO VEGETABLE SURPRISE

(I call it this because the idea for the dish came to me as I went along – and the 'surprise' bit is that it turned out to be a great success!)

Cooking time about 1 hour 10 minutes
Oven temperature Hot 220°C, 425°F, Gas Mark 7
SERVES 4

1 large onion, chopped	1 medium cauliflower
40 g/1½ oz margarine	3 medium leeks
450 g/1 lb tomatoes, skinned and roughly chopped	wholewheat breadcrumbs
1 clove garlic, crushed	225 g/8 oz crumbly cheese, such as Lancashire
3–4 spring onions, chopped	good pinch paprika
good pinch marjoram	300 ml/½ pint dry cider
pinch thyme	225 g/8 oz button mushrooms
pinch oregano	1½ tablespoons honey
salt and black pepper	

Fry the onion gently in the margarine for a few minutes until soft, then add the tomatoes. Stir in the garlic, spring onions, marjoram, thyme, oregano and salt and pepper. Bring the mixture to the boil, then simmer for about 20–30 minutes until a thickened sauce is obtained.

Meanwhile, take the whole cauliflower, with green leaves and stalk removed, and place stalk-side down in a couple of inches of salted water. Cook until tender but firm. Cut the leeks into 2.5-cm/1-inch strips and cook in boiling salted water for 5–10 minutes. Break the cauliflower into florets,

90

arrange them in a large ovenproof dish and sprinkle the leek strips on top. Season, then pour the tomato sauce mixture over the vegetables.

Cover with a layer of wholewheat breadcrumbs about 2.5–4 cm/1–1½ inches thick, then crumble the cheese evenly over the breadcrumbs. Sprinkle some paprika over the cheese and pour 150 ml/¼ pint cider over the top. Cook in a hot oven for 20–30 minutes or until the cheese is beginning to turn brown. Garnish with chopped spring onion greens.

While waiting for the main dish, place the cleaned button mushrooms in a pan, pour the remaining cider over them and stir in the honey. Cook for 5–7 minutes until the mushrooms are tender but still retaining some firmness. Serve the mushrooms in a little of the cider and honey sauce.

Serve the entire dish with either a jacket potato or some boiled (preferably new) potatoes.

KASHA
(Roast buckwheat)
Cooking time about 40 minutes
SERVES 4

225 g/8 oz unroasted
  buckwheat (dry)
1½ tablespoons vegetable
  oil

450 ml/¾ pint water
salt and pepper

Brown the buckwheat in the oil in a frying pan for 5–10 minutes (a lovely nutty aroma will rise up from the pan). Keep shaking the buckwheat until it turns a light golden colour then transfer to a saucepan containing the water. Add salt and pepper and bring to boil. Cover and simmer for about 20–30 minutes, without stirring, until the water evaporates, leaving the buckwheat swollen and cooked. (You can add a little more water if it evaporates too quickly.) Do not overcook.

Serve with button mushrooms in a cheese sauce, or eat on its own with soy sauce for a delicious protein-packed meal.

I like roast buckwheat served with plenty of soy sauce as it seems to complement the nuttiness.

BUTTER BEAN ROAST
Cooking time about 4 hours
Oven temperature Hot 220°C, 425°F, Gas Mark 7
SERVES 3

225 g/8 oz butter beans	good pinch onion salt
50 g/2 oz margarine	good pinch garlic salt
40 g/1½ oz flour	pinch nutmeg
150 ml/¼ pint milk	salt and pepper
150 ml/¼ pint bean cooking water	25 g/1 oz wholemeal breadcrumbs
good pinch celery salt	browned breadcrumbs

Soak the butter beans in plenty of water for about 3 hours, then simmer until soft. Make sure they are thoroughly cooked before mashing them.

Melt the margarine in a pan, stir in the flour then add the milk and bean water. Stir, bring to the boil then simmer for a few minutes, adding the celery, onion and garlic salts, nutmeg and salt and pepper. Mix the breadcrumbs into the mashed butter beans, then pour the sauce over, combining thoroughly. Grease and coat a cake tin with the browned breadcrumbs and add the butter bean mixture. Smooth the top and bake in a hot oven for 30–40 minutes. Turn out and serve with vegetarian gravy (see page 62) and mashed potatoes.

COURGETTE AND TOMATO QUICKIE
Cooking time 20–25 minutes
Oven temperature Moderately Hot 200°C, 400°F, Gas Mark 6
SERVES 3–4

50 g/2 oz margarine	1 400-g/14-oz can tomatoes, peeled and chopped
225 g/8 oz onions, sliced thinly	salt and black pepper
450 g/1 lb courgettes, topped and tailed	1 small stick French bread
	100 g/4 oz grated cheese

Fry the onion in half the margarine for a few minutes until soft. Slice the courgettes, add them to the onions and continue cooking for several more minutes until courgettes are softened. Add a little garlic if wished. Stir in the tomatoes and seasoning and simmer on a low light for 5 minutes. Pour into a shallow ovenproof dish.

Cut the bread into half-inch slices and spread one side with the rest of the margarine. Arrange the slices margarine side down in a layer on top of the mixture, leaving a small circle in the middle. Sprinkle the cheese over the bread, along with a little more black pepper, and bake in a moderately hot oven for about 10–15 minutes until the top is crispy.

BAKED LENTIL ROUNDS
Cooking time about 1 hour 30 minutes
Oven temperature Moderately Hot 200°C, 400°F, Gas Mark 6
SERVES 3–4

225 g/8 oz red lentils
50 g/2 oz margarine
2 cloves garlic, chopped finely
2 medium onions, chopped finely
4 large tomatoes, peeled and chopped (or 1 small can tomatoes)

4 tablespoons tomato purée
4 oz wholewheat breadcrumbs
1 teaspoon basil
salt and black pepper
1 egg

Place the lentils in a pan and cover with about half an inch of water. Bring to boil, then simmer gently until cooked (about 45 minutes to an hour) and all the water is absorbed. It might be necessary to add some water during cooking.

Fry the garlic and onions in the margarine for ten minutes in a covered pan. Add the chopped tomatoes and tomato purée and cook for 3 minutes. Stir the mixture into the cooked lentils, along with the basil, breadcrumbs, salt and pepper. Beat the egg into the mixture with a fork. Form into round shapes with your hands. Bake in moderately hot oven for about 30 minutes until brown. Serve with a green

93

vegetable, in a little tomato sauce (see recipe for spaghetti in tomato sauce page 88) if desired.

FRENCH BREAD PIZZA
Cooking time about 15–20 minutes
Oven temperature Moderately Hot 200°C, 400°F, Gas Mark 6

SERVES 2

Forget about those really expensive frozen French bread pizzas you see in the shops. Here is a quick and simple way to prepare a fresher, more tasty substitute.

Cut a French loaf to your desired length depending how hungry you are – about 8 inches should suffice. Then cut the loaf lengthways so that you have two halves of equal length and thickness.

Spread a little margarine over the bread, then a thin layer of tomato purée. Over this, add a layer of chopped tinned tomatoes (peeled and skinned). Smooth out with a knife. Sprinkle on some finely-chopped garlic (optional), then add very finely sliced onion rings along the length. Sprinkle on a smattering of basil and/or oregano, then cover with a generous helping of grated Cheddar or Lancashire cheese, as you prefer. Add lashings of black pepper, then bake in a moderately hot oven for about 15–20 minutes until the cheese is melted and bubbly and starting to turn golden brown.

Serve with a side salad or a helping of freshly-cooked sliced runner or French beans tossed in a little butter and black pepper. A glass or two of a good chianti or burgundy adds to the pleasure.

Checklist It's difficult to give precise measurements in this recipe as it all depends on how big you want your french bread pizza to be, but you will need the following.

1 French loaf	An onion
A little margarine	Basil and/or oregano
Some tomato purée	Cheese of your choice
Tinned tomatoes	Black pepper
Garlic	

SAUCY SCALLOPED POTATOES
Cooking time 45–50 minutes
SERVES 2

50 g/2 oz margarine
2 medium onions
1 clove garlic (optional)
2 carrots
100 g/4 oz mushrooms
675 g/1½ lb medium-sized
  potatoes

1 teaspoon Vecon
1 teaspoon mixed herbs
1 tablespoon tomato purée
2 tablespoons anchovy-free
  Worcestershire sauce
1 tablespoon soy sauce
salt and black pepper to taste

Melt the butter in a large frying pan, slice the onions thinly and fry until golden brown. Add the chopped garlic, thinly-sliced carrots and sliced mushrooms. Slice the potatoes thinly and add to the other ingredients in the pan. Fry for 4–5 minutes, allowing the potatoes to brown slightly but taking care not to let the mixture stick to the pan. Turn frequently. Add enough water to cover the mixture, then stir in the Vecon and remaining ingredients. Cover the pan and simmer gently for about 30 minutes or until all the ingredients are cooked. The dish will have a slightly sloppy consistency.

If you don't want the dish to be spicy, omit the Worcestershire sauce and add some washed and picked lentils (about 50 g/2 oz) when you add the water. For a smoky bacon flavour to the dish, add a handful of Smokey Snaps when you add the water.

95

COURGETTES PORTUGUAISE
Cooking time 30 minutes
SERVES 4

50 g/2 oz butter
1 large onion, chopped
  finely
1 clove garlic, crushed and
  chopped finely
2 teaspoons paprika
2 tablespoons tomato purée
1 teaspoon rosemary,
  crushed finely

½ teaspoon basil
25 g/1 oz plain flour
150 ml/¼ pint light stock
2 400-g/14-oz cans
  tomatoes, peeled and
  chopped
900 g/2 lb courgettes, sliced
salt and black pepper

Gently fry the onions and garlic in half the butter for 5–10 minutes until soft, stirring constantly. Add paprika, tomato purée, rosemary, basil and flour and cook for a few minutes before adding stock and seasoning. Add chopped tomatoes with juice and simmer for up to 15 minutes to create a thickish sauce. Meanwhile fry the courgettes in the remaining butter (adding more butter if necessary), stirring to prevent sticking. After about 10 minutes, place the courgettes in a large serving bowl, pour on the mixture and mix thoroughly.

SPROUT DE LUXE
Cooking time about 15 minutes
SERVES 2

450 g/1 lb brussels sprouts
40 g/1½ oz butter
2 medium onions
450 g/1 lb tomatoes, skinned
  and chopped (or 1 400-g/
  14-oz can)
1 clove garlic, chopped
  finely

50 g/2 oz grated Cheddar
  cheese
½ teaspoon basil
egg mixture
3 eggs
5 tablespoons water
black pepper and salt
pinch of dry mustard

Prepare the sprouts, then cook in a little salted water for 10 minutes or until cooked. In the meantime, chop the onions

finely and cook in the melted butter in a frying pan for a
few minutes until tender. Add the tomatoes and garlic and
continue to cook for several minutes. Drain the sprouts and
toss them in a little butter, then add to the frying pan mixture.

Beat the egg mixture thoroughly, then add to the frying
pan, stirring thoroughly. Sprinkle on the cheese, the basil
and some freshly grated black pepper and allow the mixture
to thicken.

Serve hot with fresh garden peas.

. This also makes a good savoury supper dish.

LENTIL AND EGG CURRY
Cooking time about 45 minutes
SERVES 3–4

40 g/1½ oz margarine	200 g/7 oz red split lentils
1 large onion, peeled and chopped finely	600 ml stock
1 clove garlic (optional), chopped finely	1½ tablespoons tomato purée
1½–2 tablespoons curry powder (or to taste)	salt and pepper
	4 hard-boiled eggs, sliced
	parsley to garnish

Fry the onion and garlic in the margarine for a few minutes
until soft, then stir in the curry powder and fry for a minute
or so. Add the lentils, stock, purée and seasoning. Bring to
the boil for a couple of minutes, then simmer gently for
around 40 minutes until lentils are soft-cooked. Pour into a
serving dish, arrange the egg slices on top and sprinkle with
parsley. Accompany with brown rice.

RAJAH RICE AND VEGETABLE CURRY
Cooking time 45–50 minutes
SERVES 2–3

75 g/3 oz margarine
2 medium onions, finely
chopped
1 clove garlic, finely
chopped
1–2 tablespoons curry
powder (or to taste)
175 g/6 oz brown rice,
washed

600 ml/1 pint stock
450 g/1 lb garden peas
(unshelled weight)
50 g/2 oz French beans,
topped and tailed and cut
into ½-inch pieces
100 g/4 oz mushrooms

Melt half the margarine in a large saucepan and add the onions and garlic. Fry for 10–15 minutes until soft, stirring frequently. Stir in the curry powder and fry for a further 2 minutes. Stir in the rice, then add the stock. Bring to boil and simmer gently for 15 minutes. Add the peas and beans. Cook till soft. You may need to adjust the mixture with water or stock.

Meanwhile, start to fry the mushrooms in the rest of the margarine. When the peas and beans are soft, add the mushrooms, stir well and serve with spicy poppadoms and a little mango chutney.

For extra texture, sprinkle a few roasted sunflower seeds over the top.

TOMATO PIE
Cooking time 35 minutes
Oven temperature Moderate 180°C, 350°F, Gas Mark 4
SERVES 4

40 g/1½ oz butter
450 g/1 lb onions
900 g/2 lb plump tomatoes
(or 2 400-g/14-oz cans)
175 g/6 oz fresh wholewheat
breadcrumbs

2 free range eggs
2 tablespoons chopped fresh
parsley
1 teaspoon basil
salt and black pepper

Peel and slice the onions thinly and fry in the butter until soft. Skin the fresh tomatoes by placing in boiling water for a few seconds, then into cold water (or use the canned tomatoes). Chop finely and stir into the onions. Cook for 5 minutes. Put the wholewheat breadcrumbs and herbs into a bowl, mix together and bind with the eggs. Mix together the tomato/onion mixture and the breadcrumbs, then season. Put in a greased ovenproof dish and bake in a moderate oven for 15 minutes. Serve with a green vegetable.

LEEK AND MACARONI AU GRATIN
Cooking time about 45 minutes
Oven temperature Moderately Hot 190°C, 375°F, Gas Mark 5
SERVES 3–4

175 g/6 oz macaroni
60 g/2½ oz margarine
1 medium onion, finely chopped
1 clove garlic, finely chopped (optional)
350 g/12 oz leeks, washed, topped and tailed

40 g/1½ oz plain flour
750 ml/1¼ pint milk
275 g/10 oz Lancashire cheese, grated
salt and black pepper
175 g/6 oz wholewheat breadcrumbs

Boil the macaroni for about 10 minutes until cooked. Drain and dry off excess water.

Fry the onions and garlic together in the margarine for a few minutes, then add the leeks and fry for another 3–4 minutes. Stir frequently. Add the flour and stir in for about a minute. Remove from heat and add the milk, then bring gradually to the boil until the sauce is thick. Remove from heat and add the cheese, keeping back 8 tablespoons. Add the macaroni and season to taste.

Put the mixture into a greased shallow ovenproof dish. Mix the breadcrumbs and the rest of the cheese together and sprinkle on top. Bake in a moderately hot oven for about half an hour until golden brown.

SAVOURY POT BARLEY* WITH MUSHROOMS

Cooking time about 50 minutes

SERVES 4

*Pot barley is another name for whole-grain brown barley. It has a higher nutritional content than pearl barley, containing more protein, calcium and iron . . . although you could use pearl barley in this recipe if there was no pot barley in stock.

175 g/6 oz pot barley
50 g/2 oz margarine
2 medium onions, peeled and finely chopped
1 chopped clove garlic (optional)
1 thinly sliced leek (optional)

225 g/8 oz mushrooms, sliced
1 tablespoon tomato purée
2 tablespoons soy sauce
1 teaspoon Marmite
¼ teaspoon basil or parsley
black pepper, lots to taste.

Roast the barley in a pan containing ½ oz margarine, stirring all the time.

Melt the rest of the margarine in another large pan, add the onions, garlic, leek and sliced mushrooms and fry until soft (about 10 minutes). Stir in the tomato purée, soy sauce and Marmite, then add the barley. Add enough water to cover, along with herbs and seasoning. Bring to boil and simmer for about 45 minutes until the barley is soft, adding water as necessary as it is absorbed. Aim for a consistency which is neither sloppy nor sticky.

When cooked, sprinkle with a little soy sauce to taste and serve with, say, a jacket potato and a green vegetable such as broccoli. This is a very wholesome, ribsticking meal.

SPICY SOYA BEAN STEW
Cooking time up to 3 hours
SERVES 4

175 g/6 oz soya beans (dry weight)
40 g/1½ oz margarine
2 large onions, peeled and chopped finely
50 g/2 oz mushrooms sliced
2 sticks celery, thinly sliced
2 carrots, thinly sliced
2 400-g/ 14-oz tins of tomatoes

5 tablespoons tomato purée
1 teaspoon parsley
½ teaspoon basil
½ teaspoon oregano
½ teaspoon chilli powder
2 teaspoons Vecon
12 strands wholewheat spaghetti
salt and black pepper

Soak the beans overnight, allowing plenty of water to cover as the beans expand in size. Drain and place the beans in a large pan. Cover with 2 inches of water, boil for 10 minutes and then simmer on a low light for 2–3 hours, stirring occasionally and topping up with a little water when necessary. When cooked, drain, reserving half the liquid for later.

Melt the margarine in a large pan. Add the garlic and fry gently for about a minute, then add onions and fry for 5–10 minutes. Add the mushrooms, celery and carrot and braise together in a covered pan for 10 minutes, stirring from time to time. Chop the tomatoes, discarding any stalks or skin, and add with the tomato juice to the pan. Cook for 10 minutes and add the tomato purée. Stir in the herbs, chilli powder and Vecon. Add the beans, along with a little of the bean stock, and break the spaghetti into the mixture. Season with lots of black pepper to taste. Simmer gently on a low light for about 20 minutes or longer to allow the beans and spices to mix. Then serve.

Note: This is a very substantial, thick, warming winter-type dish which can be equally tasty in summer if you perhaps omit the chilli and add sliced courgettes, French or runner beans instead.

TVP – MEATLESS MEAT MEALS

(For people who'd rather not give up meat.)
If this sounds a little confusing, let me explain. Thanks to a wide range of textured vegetable proteins (TVP) now available, you can still eat some of your favourite meat dishes, should you wish – with these added bonuses:
* Food bills are cut.
* TVP contains less calorie content than meat.
* There's no animal fat and no gristle to put you off eating it.

Life has never been easier for people who want to become vegetarian or vegan. You don't have to give up your hot pots, cottage pies, pasties, beefburgers, meat and potato pies – or whatever it is that turns your stomach juices on.

TVP gives more protein and less calories than steak, weight for weight, and when constituted has a fat content of less than one per cent – against an average of five per cent for lean meat.

But a word of warning – I personally have found that a few of the packaged and canned meat substitute convenience meals on the market are enough to turn the staunchest vegetarian to eating meat. Quite frankly, after non-vegetarian friends of mine have tried out these products through sheer curiosity, they've said 'If *that's* what vegetarians eat, they're welcome to it!'

Of course, not everything from a can is inedible – some meat substitute products are very appetising. But it largely remains a case of trial and error, and personal taste. Try some of the products if you wish but prepare, in some cases, to be disappointed. But don't let it put you off becoming a vegetarian. By far the best way is to buy TVP loose from the health food shop – or in packets – and make your own meals from some of the recipes that follow.

To reconstitute TVP Add two parts *by weight* of hot water to one part of TVP mince and leave for about 4 minutes. For example, use 250 ml/8 fl oz water to 100 g/4 oz TVP. Stir in a teaspoonful of yeast extract (such as Vecon or Marmite) and let it soak through. Add pepper to taste, for extra flavour. If you use cold water, leave for 15 minutes. A quick way to

102

measure is 1 cup water to 1 cup TVP. TVP chunks take longer, according to manufacturers' instructions.
Note: Treat reconstituted TVP like fresh meat – eat at once or refrigerate.

MEAT AND POTATO PIE
Cooking time 40 minutes
Oven temperature Moderately Hot 190°C, 375°F, Gas Mark 5
SERVES 3–4

225 g/8 oz wholewheat
  shortcrust pastry
1 kg/2 lb potatoes
2 medium onions, finely
  chopped

4 tablespoons dry TVP
  mince, reconstituted
salt and pepper
garlic salt

Roll out half the pastry to 5 mm/¼ inch thick and use to line a 20-cm/8-inch ovenproof plate. Cook the potatoes and onions together until soft. Drain and add the reconstituted TVP. Stir and mash together until smooth. Add salt and pepper and a little garlic salt. Pile the filling on to the pastry base and spread evenly. Cover with the other half of the pastry and seal the edges. Bake in a moderately hot oven for 20 minutes.

CORNISH PASTIES
Cooking time 45 minutes
Oven temperature Hot 220°C, 425°F, Gas Mark 7
MAKES 2 PASTIES

225 g/8 oz shortcrust pastry
450 g/1 lb potatoes, cut into
  pieces
2 medium onions, chopped
2 medium carrots, sliced

2 tablespoons dry TVP
  mince, reconstituted
salt and pepper
little garlic salt

Roll out the pastry to 5-mm/¼-inch thick and cut out two round pieces using a saucer. Cook the potatoes, onions and carrots until soft. Drain and add the TVP mince. Stir and mash together well, adding salt and pepper and a little garlic salt. Place half the mixture into each pastry circle. Moisten the edges with water, fold the pastry over and press the edges together. Bake in a hot oven for 25 minutes.

MOUSSAKA
Cooking time about 45 minutes
Oven temperature Moderately Hot 190°C, 375°F, Gas Mark 5
SERVES 4

50 g/2 oz margarine
350 g/12 oz reconstituted
  TVP mince (using 100 g/
  4 oz TVP and 250 ml/8 fl
  oz water)
225 g/8 oz onions, chopped
2 tablespoons fresh parsley,
  chopped

225 g/8 oz tomatoes, skinned
  and chopped
salt and pepper
675 g/1½ lb potatoes,
  cooked

Melt the margarine and fry the TVP mince, onion, parsley and tomatoes. Add the seasoning. Slice the potatoes thinly, then place a layer of potatoes in the bottom of a baking dish. Put some of the fried TVP mixture on top. Add another layer of potatoes, followed by another layer of TVP mix and so on, finishing with a layer of potato on top.

Bake in a moderately hot oven for about 30 minutes until the top layer is golden brown. Serve topped with cheese sauce (see page 63) and green vegetables.

COTTAGE PIE
Cooking time 25 minutes
Oven temperature Moderately Hot 190°C, 375°F, Gas Mark 5
SERVES 4

2 onions, finely chopped
40 g/1½ oz margarine
350 g/12 oz reconstituted
   TVP mince (using 100 g/
   4 oz TVP and 250 ml/8 fl
   oz water)
3 tablespoons flour

1 tablespoon tomato purée
450 ml/¾ pint water
salt and pepper
675 g/1½ lb mashed
   potatoes
25 g/1 oz cheese, grated

Slowly fry the onions in the margarine until they are transparent. Add the TVP mixed with the flour and tomato purée, and stir in the water. Season. Bring slowly to the boil, stirring, and simmer for 3 minutes. Pour the mixture into a heated ovenproof dish. Cover with the prepared mashed potatoes. Sprinkle the grated cheese on top and bake or grill until lightly browned.

Serve with pickled beetroot. You can, if you wish, add a teaspoon or two of Marmite and some garlic salt.

CHILLI CON CARNE
Cooking time 1 hour
SERVES 4–6

450 g/1 lb reconstituted TVP
   mince
1 tablespoon cooking oil
1 large onion, chopped
1 green pepper, chopped
3 teaspoons chilli powder

1 396-g/14-oz can tomatoes
1 tablespoon vinegar
1 teaspoon sugar
salt and pepper
1 432-g/15¼-oz can red
   kidney beans

Fry the TVP mince in the oil with the onion and green pepper for about 5 minutes, stirring. Add the chilli powder, tomatoes, vinegar and sugar. Season with salt and pepper. Bring to the boil, stirring well, then cover and simmer for 45 minutes. Add the kidney beans and heat through. Serve with boiled rice.

MEAT PIE
Cooking time 35 minutes
Oven temperature Hot 220°C, 475°F, Gas Mark 7
SERVES 3–4

225 g/8 oz wholewheat
  shortcrust pastry
1 large onion
10 tablespoons dry TVP
  mince, reconstituted

salt and pepper
garlic salt

Roll out half the pastry to 5 mm/¼ inch thick and use to line the base of a 20-cm/8-inch pie plate.

Boil the onion until soft, then chop finely and mix with the TVP. Add salt, pepper and garlic salt, and spread the mixture evenly over the pastry base. Cover with the other half of the pastry and bake in a hot oven for about 20 minutes. Serve the pie with vegetarian gravy (see page 62), new potatoes and/or mushy peas and pickles.

CHARLIE'S CURRY
Cooking time 45 minutes
SERVES 4

2 onions, chopped
3 tablespoons oil
2 tablespoons curry powder
1 tablespoon curry paste
900 g/2 lb reconstituted TVP
  mince
1 tablespoon tomato purée
50 g/2 oz flour

1 teaspoon salt
475 ml/16 fl oz water
few sultanas
grated rind and juice of ½
  lemon
2 apples, diced
2 tomatoes, chopped
350 g/12 oz rice

Fry the onion in the oil for 5 minutes, then stir in the curry powder and paste. Cook slowly for 5 minutes. Stir in the TVP mince, tomato purée, flour and salt. Gradually pour in the water and bring to the boil. Add the sultanas, lemon rind and juice, apple and tomatoes. Adjust the seasoning and allow to simmer for 15–20 minutes. Serve on the bed of boiled rice with side dishes, if liked.

Note: Add 1 teaspoon Marmite, if required.

POTATO BEEF PIE
Cooking time 1 hour 20 minutes
Oven temperature Hot 220°C, 425°F, Gas Mark 7
SERVES 4

1 medium onion, sliced
1 tablespoon oil
225 g/8 oz beef-flavoured
  TVP chunks,
  reconstituted

150 ml/¼ pint stock
225 g/8 oz potatoes, cubed
salt and pepper
50 g/2 oz mushrooms, sliced
225 g/8 oz shortcrust pastry
little milk

Fry the onion in the oil until browned. Add the TVP chunks, stock, potatoes and season with salt and pepper. Simmer gently for 45 minutes, then transfer to a pie dish and add the mushrooms. Roll out the pastry and use to cover the pie dish. Brush the pastry with a little milk, make two slits in the centre to allow steam to escape and cook in a hot oven for 30 minutes.

BAKED POTATO WITH SAVOURY MINCE
Cooking time about 25 minutes
SERVES 1

100 g/4 oz reconstituted
  TVP mince
1 teaspoon oil
1 teaspoon concentrated
  curry sauce

4–5 tablespoons water
1½ teaspoons dried mixed
  vegetables
1 baked potato

Fry the TVP mince in the oil until well browned. Add the curry sauce, water and dried mixed vegetables. Bring to the boil and simmer, covered, for 15 minutes.

Cut a slice from the top of the baked potato and scoop out the inside. Mix with the hot TVP mixture and pile back into the potato case to serve.

DEVONSHIRE OVALS
Cooking time 10–12 minutes
MAKES 6

450 g/1 lb reconstituted TVP
  mince
2 medium onions, finely
  grated
4 medium potatoes, finely
  grated

2 eggs
juice of ½ lemon
2 teaspoons breadcrumbs
salt and pepper

Mix the TVP mince, onions and potatoes together. Separate
the eggs, add the yolks to the mixture with the lemon juice,
breadcrumbs and seasoning. Shape into ovals.

Lightly beat the egg whites and use to brush the Devon-
shire ovals. Deep fry for at least 10 minutes until cooked and
golden brown.

LOBBY
Cooking time 40 minutes
SERVES 4

1 kg/2 lb potatoes
225 g/8 oz carrots
water
2 large onions, sliced
2–3 tablespoons dry TVP
  mince

1 teaspoon Marmite
salt and pepper
garlic salt

Cut the potatoes into 2.5-cm/1-inch cubes and thinly slice
the carrots. Place in a pan and add salted water to come 2.5
cm/1 inch above the vegetables. After 10 minutes cooking
time, add the onions, TVP mince and Marmite. Turn down
the heat to just simmering and cook gently for 20 minutes
until a sloppy consistency is obtained. Season.

If liked, add a few wholewheat dumplings (see page 109).

WHOLEWHEAT DUMPLINGS
Cooking time 20 minutes
MAKES ABOUT 10 SMALL DUMPLINGS

75 g/3 oz margarine
225 g/8 oz wholewheat flour
1 teaspoon mixed herbs,
  fresh if possible

1 onion, finely chopped
½ teaspoon baking powder
6 tablespoons water

Rub the margarine into the flour. Mix in the herbs and chopped onion, then stir in the baking powder. Mix in the water and form into about 10 small balls. If too sticky, roll in a little flour. Drop into boiling water or a stew etc. and boil for 20 minutes.

BEEFBURGERS
Cooking time 40 minutes
Oven temperature Moderately Hot 190°C, 375°F, Gas Mark 5
MAKES 4 BEEFBURGERS

8 tablespoons dry TVP
  mince
1 large onion, finely
  chopped

1 small egg
1 tablespoon mixed herbs
salt and pepper

Put the TVP mince and onion in a small pan. Cover with water and simmer for about 10 minutes until most of the water is absorbed. Mix in the egg, herbs, salt and pepper. Bind together to make 4 beefburgers. Place on a baking tray and bake in a moderately hot oven for 30 minutes, turning after 15 minutes.

SHEPHERD'S MACARONI PIE
Cooking time 50–55 minutes
Oven temperature Moderately Hot 190°C, 375°F, Gas Mark 5
SERVES 4

350 g/12 oz reconstituted TVP mince (ie using 100 g/4 oz TVP and 250 ml/8 fl oz water into which 1 teaspoon Vecon has been stirred)
40 g/1½ oz margarine
2 medium onions, chopped finely
1 clove garlic, chopped finely
1 400-g/14-oz can tomatoes, peeled and chopped
1 tablespoon tomato purée
salt and black pepper
½ teaspoon oregano (optional)
1 heaped tablespoon plain flour
300 ml/½ pint stock
225 g/8 oz cooked macaroni
600 ml/1 pint cheese sauce

Melt the butter in a large saucepan and fry the onion and garlic for 5–10 minutes until soft. Stir in the mince and fry for a further 5 minutes, stirring constantly. Add the tomatoes, purée, seasoning and oregano. Stir in the flour and cook for a couple of minutes, then add the stock. Cook for 30 minutes.

Meanwhile, make the macaroni cheese.

When the mince mixture is cooked, spoon it into an oven-proof bowl, then place the macaroni cheese on top, smoothing with a knife. Bake for 15 minutes in a moderately hot oven.

Note: In place of making up the macaroni cheese yourself, you may if you prefer use a large can of macaroni cheese.

Vegetables, Salads and Sprouting Dishes

Let's start with the potato. I wonder why we always label it 'the humble potato . . .?' How dare we append such a lowly tag to a noble part of creation bearing regal titles such as: King Edward, Ulster Sceptre, Maris Peer, Majestic, Pentland Crown and Reds Craig Royal.

Perhaps it's because the potato is shapeless, earthy, common, lumpy and dumpy in its natural form that leads us to malign it.

Potatoes have an undeserved reputation as being a fattening food when, plain boiled they are a mere 23 calories per 25 g/ 1 oz and contain protein, Vitamin C and a selection of other vitamins and minerals.

Early new potatoes are usually available in late May and in June, July and August and taste better when fresh. You can tell if they're fresh, if the skin comes easily away when you rub the potato gently with your finger. Never store new potatoes for more than a day or so.

Maincrop potatoes are usually available from September through until May.

With a little effort, you can become a potato connoisseur and discover which potato lends itself best to the dishes you enjoy.

For instance, best for *boiling and mashing* are King Edwards, Desirée (Reds), Maris Piper, Pentland Hawk and Pentland Ivory (Whites).

For *chips and sauté potatoes*, use King Edward, Desirée, Majestic, Maris Piper or Pentland Ivory.

Pentland Crown, Maris Piper, Pentland Hawk (White), King Edward and Desirée make the best *roast and jacket potatoes*.

And for *new potatoes and potato salads*, the best to use are Reds Craig Royal (Red), Maris Peer and Ulster Sceptre (White).

I must confess that if there was an appreciation society on behalf of potatoes, I'd be the first to join.

So here are some delicious and filling recipes that prove there's more than meets the eye when it comes to a sack of spuds. It's Goodbye Mr Chips and Hello King Edward . . .

POTATO POINTERS

* Peel potatoes thinly to conserve the nutrients.
* Store potatoes in a cool dark place where air can circulate.
* When boiling potatoes, cook them in only enough water to prevent them sticking. Retain the cooking water for making thick stock, soups and sauces.
* Potatoes are cooked if they are easy to prick with a fork but still firm.
* Steamed, pressure-cooked or boiled in their jackets – potatoes retain more of their nutritive value when cooked like this than in any other method.
* Peeling potatoes a long time ahead of cooking, or leaving potatoes standing after cooking, may cause them to lose some of their nutrients.
* In cooked potatoes, the loss of Vitamin C is greater if the vegetables are mashed and kept hot than if they are kept whole under similar conditions. It is better to reheat potatoes than keep them hot.
* If bought in a polythene bag, open the bag to prevent the potatoes 'sweating'. Better still, transfer them to a vegetable rack.
* If, as happens in some seasons, potatoes go mushy on cooking, try boiling very gently or steaming.

MASHED AND BOILED POTATO VARIATIONS

Duchesse After drying boiled potatoes over a low heat, mash thoroughly or press through a sieve to remove any lumps. Add a little butter, seasoning and 1 egg to every 450 g/1 lb potatoes. Beat well. Spoon the mixture into a piping bag fitted with a large star nozzle and pipe in swirls or pyramids on to a greased baking sheet.
To cook: Bake in a hot oven at 220°C, 425°F, Gas Mark 7 for

about 10–15 minutes until lightly browned. The potatoes may be brushed lightly with beaten egg before serving.

To serve: Serve hot, garnished with chopped parsley or parsley sprigs. This mixture may also be used for potato nests, croquettes or as a piped border for TVP, egg or savoury dishes.

Croquettes Use the same mixture as for Duchesse potatoes. With floured hands, roll into cork shapes and brush with beaten egg. Coat with browned breadcrumbs.

To cook: Fry in hot deep oil for 3–4 minutes until golden brown. Drain well on absorbent kitchen paper.

To serve: Serve hot with TVP or savoury dishes.

Note: Finely chopped parsley, minced onion or chopped hard-boiled egg may be added to the croquette mixture.

Saute Potatoes Peel the potatoes thinly and parboil in salted water for about 10 minutes. Drain well and dry off in the pan over a low heat. (This reduces the moisture content and prevents spluttering during the final cooking.) Cut the potatoes into thick slices.

To cook: Heat butter or oil in frying pan, add the sliced potatoes. Fry gently on both sides until crisped, brown and thoroughly cooked. Shake the pan occasionally to ensure even browning.

To serve: Serve hot, sprinkled with salt and finely chopped parsley. They can be served mixed with green peppers, chopped and cooked, sliced fried onions or sliced fried mushrooms.

New Potatoes Wash and scrub the potatoes.

To cook: Cook in the boiling salted water with a sprig of mint added for about 15–20 minutes. Drain well and dry over a low heat.

To serve: Toss in melted butter and serve sprinkled with chopped fresh parsley, mint, chives or watercress. Or coat the boiled potatoes with a cheese, parsley or mustard sauce.

POTATO DOUGHNUTS
Cooking time 5–7 minutes
SERVES 3–4

100 g/4 oz plain flour
1½ teaspoons baking
  powder
pinch cinnamon
50 g/2 oz butter

castor sugar
50 g/2 oz cooked potato,
  sieved
1 egg, beaten
oil for deep frying

Sieve the flour, baking powder and cinnamon together. Rub in the butter until it resembles fine breadcrumbs. Add 1 teaspoon castor sugar to the mixture, then blend in the potato with the beaten egg to make a stiff dough. Roll out to about 1 cm/½ inch thick on a floured board. Using a 7.5–10-cm/ 3–4-inch cutter, stamp out rounds, then using a cutter, cut out the centres.

Deep fry the doughnuts for 5–7 minutes until golden brown, then drain and sprinkle liberally with castor sugar.

FANCY DRESSED EGGHILLS
SERVES 4

225 g/8 oz potatoes, cooked
  and diced
½ cucumber, diced
3 carrots, grated
75 g/3 oz cheese, diced
about 2 tablespoons oil and
  vinegar dressing

4 hard-boiled eggs
8 teaspoons mayonnaise
paprika
watercress sprigs to garnish

Mix the potatoes, cucumber, carrot and cheese with the dressing and place in a serving dish.

Cut the eggs in half lengthwise and place over the salad. Coat each egg with mayonnaise and sprinkle with paprika. Garnish with watercress sprigs.

POTATO SCOTTIES
Cooking time about 10 minutes
MAKES 4 SCOTTIES

225 g/8 oz mashed potatoes   4 hard-boiled eggs
1 egg, slightly beaten   browned breadcrumbs
salt and pepper

Beat the mashed potato and half the raw egg together and season well. Surround each hard-boiled egg with the potato. Coat with the remainder of the raw egg and roll in the browned breadcrumbs. Deep fry for about 10 minutes until golden brown.

POTATO FLATTIES
Cooking time 10–15 minutes
SERVES 4

450 g/1 lb potatoes   1 tablespoon self-raising
1 medium onion   flour
1 egg   oil for shallow frying
salt and pepper

Grate the potatoes coarsely, pouring off any water. Grate or chop the onion and mix with the potato. Add the egg, salt and pepper and bind with the flour, stirring in a little more if necessary. Fry tablespoons of the mixture in shallow oil for about 10–15 minutes, turning after 5 minutes. Drain thoroughly on absorbent kitchen paper and serve hot.

Two or three flatties can be sandwiched together with grated cheese, cooked sliced mushrooms, fried tomatoes, or with apple, if you have a sweet tooth.

QUICK CURRY SAUTÉ POTATOES
Cooking time 20 minutes
SERVES 4

450 g/1 lb potatoes   25 g/1 oz butter
about 1 tablespoon curry
   powder, according to
   strength and taste

115

Parboil the potatoes in salted water for about 10 minutes. Drain, return the potatoes to the pan and gently dry over a low heat. Cut into thickish slices and coat with the curry powder. Fry in the butter, turning occasionally. Serve hot.

POTATO EGG COSIES
Cooking time 1 hour 25 minutes
Oven temperature Moderately Hot 200°C, 400°F; Gas Mark 6
SERVES 4

4 225–275-g/8–10-oz potatoes, scrubbed and pricked	salt and pepper
	4 hard-boiled eggs
	4 slices processed cheese
25 g/1 oz butter	

Put the potatoes on a baking sheet and bake in a moderately hot oven for 1¼ hours. When cooked, cut the potatoes in half lengthwise. Scoop out the centres, taking care not to break the skin. Mix the butter and seasoning into the potato. Return the mixture to each potato shell and smooth the tops. Cut the eggs in half lengthwise and place a half, cut side down, on each potato. Cover with half a cheese slice, tucking the corners into the potato. Return to the oven for 5–10 minutes, then serve.

CREAMY POTATO RELISH
Cooking time 10 minutes
SERVES 4

450 g/1 lb cooked potatoes	4 tablespoons salad cream
4 tablespoons relish or chutney	1 tablespoon vinegar
	salt to taste

Cut the potatoes into small dice. Place in a saucepan and add the rest of the ingredients. Warm through gently. Serve as accompaniment to eggs or meatless sausages.

CREOLE POTATOES
Cooking time 25 minutes
SERVES 4

450 g/1 lb potatoes
25 g/1 oz butter
1 onion, thinly sliced
3 tablespoons tomato
  ketchup

1 teaspoon Worcestershire
  sauce
salt

Parboil the potatoes in salted water for about 10 minutes.
Drain, return the potatoes to the saucepan and dry over a
low heat. Cut into thick slices.

Melt the butter in a frying pan and add the onion and
potatoes. Cook until lightly browned, turning occasionally.
Add the tomato ketchup, Worcestershire sauce and salt. Mix
well together and serve hot.

LEMON POTATO PUFFLES
Cooking time 9 minutes
SERVES 4

450 g/1 lb potatoes
for the marinade
8 tablespoons olive oil
4 tablespoons white wine
  vinegar
black pepper
pinch salt
pinch castor sugar
2 teaspoons grated lemon
  rind

for the fritter batter
100 g/4 oz plain flour
½ teaspoon salt
pepper
150 ml/¼ pint lukewarm
  water
1 tablespoon melted butter
2 egg whites, stiffly beaten
dried or chopped fresh
  herbs, if liked

Cut the potatoes in 5-mm/¼-inch slices and parboil for about
3 minutes. Drain and place in a shallow dish. Stir the marinade ingredients together and pour over the potatoes. Leave
for 1 hour.

Sift the flour into a bowl and add the seasoning. Mix in
the water and butter, then fold in the egg whites. Add the

herbs, if used. Dip each potato slice into the batter, using a fork, and shake to remove any excess batter. Deep fry for 6 minutes and drain on absorbent kitchen paper.

DICEY POTATOES
Cooking time about 20 minutes
SERVES 4

25 g/1 oz butter	salt
1 clove garlic, crushed	chopped fresh parsley to
2 tablespoons oil	garnish
450 g/1 lb potatoes, cut into	
1-cm/½-inch cubes	

Heat the butter, garlic and oil in a pan, add the potatoes and fry gently until cooked and golden brown. Drain on absorbent kitchen paper. Sprinkle with salt and garnish with chopped parsley.

POTATO LORRAINE
Cooking time 30 minutes
Oven temperature Moderately Hot 190°C, 375°F, Gas Mark 5
SERVES 4

225 g/8 oz boiled potatoes	salt and pepper
50 g/2 oz cheese, grated	nutmeg to taste
2 eggs	25 g/1 oz butter
2 tablespoons milk	

Slice the potatoes to about 5 mm/¼ inch thick. Sprinkle half the cheese into a greased pie dish and cover evenly with the potato slices.

Beat the eggs, milk, salt, pepper and nutmeg together and pour into the pie dish. Sprinkle with the remaining cheese, dot with the butter and cook in a moderately hot oven for 30 minutes.

SCRUNCHY SPECIALS (from Lancashire)
Cooking time about 5 minutes
SERVES 4

100 g/4 oz flour
1 egg
150 ml/¼ pint milk

drop of vinegar
3–4 medium potatoes

Mix the flour and egg with the milk and beat to make a smooth batter. Add the vinegar. Slice the potatoes thinly and dip each slice in the batter mixture, covering well and shaking off the excess batter. Deep fry for about 5 minutes until golden brown.

★ ★ ★

TO COOK ASPARAGUS

Scrape the asparagus stalks and trim the ends if tough and woody. Wash the asparagus and tie together in manageable bunches of about 8–10 spears, depending on size. Stand the bunches upright in a saucepan and add enough boiling salted water to cover the stalk ends. The heads of the asparagus should be above water. Cover the pan and cook gently for 15–20 minutes until tender. Overcooked asparagus becomes watery and loses its flavour. Drain carefully and serve with melted butter or hollandaise sauce.

HERBED BEANS
Cooking time 15 minutes
SERVES 4

450 g/1 lb green beans
1 small onion, chopped
15 g/½ oz batter
1 tablespoon chopped fresh
 tarragon or 1 teaspoon
 dried

2 tablespoons single cream
 or top of the milk
salt and pepper
pinch grated nutmeg

Cook the green beans in boiling salted water for about 15 minutes and drain thoroughly. Meanwhile, fry the onion gently in the butter. Stir in the chopped fresh or dried tarragon, cream or top of the milk and seasonings. Pour over the beans and serve.

BATTERED BROCCOLI
Cooking time 4–5 minutes
SERVES 4

450 g/1 lb broccoli   oil for deep frying
300 ml/½ pint coating   grated Parmesan
  batter (see page 64)

Break the broccoli into florets. Rinse well in salted water, drain and dry. Dip into the coating batter and deep fry for 4–5 minutes until crisp and golden brown. Drain on absorbent kitchen paper. Place in a heated serving dish and sprinkle with grated Parmesan cheese.

CABBAGE WITH BURNT ORANGE SAUCE
Cooking time 30 minutes
SERVES 3–4

½ medium cabbage   1 tablespoon marmalade
juice of 1 orange   2 tablespoons brown sugar
knob of butter or margarine juice of ½ lemon
salt and pepper

Finely shred the cabbage and put in a pan with the orange juice and knob of butter or margarine. Season to taste, then cover the pan and cook gently for 10–15 minutes. Drain the cabbage thoroughly, reserving the cooking liquid, and keep warm.

Boil the cooking liquid until reduced by half, then stir in the marmalade, brown sugar and lemon juice. Bring to the boil and simmer for a few minutes. Toss the cooked cabbage in the orange sauce.

CAULIFLOWER NIÇOISE
Cooking time about 25 minutes
SERVES 4

1 onion, chopped	1 clove garlic, crushed
25 g/1 oz butter	1 tablespoon tomato purée
2 tablespoons oil	salt and pepper
225 g/8 oz tomatoes, skinned and chopped	150 ml/¼ pint stock
juice of 1 lemon	1 small cauliflower, broken into florets

Fry the onion gently in the butter and oil until beginning to soften. Add the chopped tomatoes, lemon juice, crushed garlic, tomato purée, seasoning and stock. Stir and bring to the boil, adding the cauliflower florets. Cover the pan and simmer gently until the cauliflower is just tender.

* * *

HOW TO SERVE CELERIAC

If you like celery. I must urge you to try this delicious stable-mate. It looks something like a small turnip but the delicate flavour is very refreshing.

First peel the celeriac, then grate into a bowl and pour on a simple dressing of 4 tablespoons corn oil mixed with 2 tablespoons lemon juice, salt and black pepper. It's best to eat the celeriac more or less immediately once the dressing has been mixed in as it may go slightly soggy.

You can also eat celeriac in salads or as a tasty topping on a TVP beefburger (see page 109) between bread.

CELERY PROVENÇALE
Cooking time 35 minutes
SERVES 6–8

2 bunches of celery	salt and pepper
1 tablespoon oil	½ teaspoon ground coriander
2 cloves garlic, crushed	
1 396-g/14-oz can tomatoes	1 teaspoon tomato purée

Chop the celery coarsely. Heat the oil and fry the garlic and onion until just turning brown. Add the celery and fry for 1 minute, then add the tomatoes with their juice, salt, pepper and coriander. Cover and simmer for 15 minutes. Stir in the tomato purée and cook for a further 5 minutes.

CUCUMBER SAMBAL
SERVES 4

1 cucumber	150 ml/¼ pint natural
salt	yogurt
pinch garlic salt	1 tablespoon chopped fresh
black pepper	parsley or mixed herbs

Slice the cucumber, place in a colander and sprinkle liberally with salt. Leave to drain for 30 minutes. Rinse off the excess salt and place in a bowl. Mix with the garlic salt, black pepper and yogurt. Stir in the chopped parsley or mixed herbs.

CUCUMBER WITH LEMON SAUCE
Cooking time 15 minutes
SERVES 4

1 cucumber	½ teaspoon castor sugar
little stock	salt and pepper
150 ml/¼ pint single cream	chopped fresh parsley to
grated rind of 1 lemon	garnish

Peel the cucumber, cut into cubes and salt as in the previous recipe. Put in a shallow pan with a little stock to cover. Cover the pan and simmer for 10 minutes. Drain the cucumber and keep warm. Heat 2 tablespoons of the stock gently with the cream, grated lemon rind, castor sugar, salt and pepper to taste. Stir the cucumber into the sauce and serve sprinkled with chopped parsley.

CUCUMBER CURRY
Cooking time 20 minutes
SERVES 4

1 cucumber
1 teaspoon curry powder

150 ml/¼ pint double cream
salt and pepper

Dice the cucumber into 2.5-cm/1-inch cubes. Blanch in boiling salted water for 5–10 minutes until just tender. Drain. Add the curry powder to the double cream a little at a time, stirring constantly, until a thin paste forms. Mix the curried cream and cucumber together. Season and heat gently for 10 minutes.

LEMON MARROW
Cooking time 10 minutes
SERVES 4

1 small marrow
50 g/2 oz butter
grated rind and juice of 1 lemon
1 tablespoon sugar

2 tablespoons chopped fresh parsley
1 teaspoon dill seeds
salt and pepper

Halve the marrow, remove the centre seeds and soft fibres. Cut the marrow into cubes, without peeling. Heat the butter and add the marrow, grated lemon rind, sugar, chopped parsley and dill seeds. Add salt and pepper to taste. Cover and cook gently for 8–10 minutes. Squeeze in the lemon juice and serve.

GLAZED ONIONS or NEW POTATOES
Cooking time about 30 minutes
SERVES 4

450 g/1 lb small onions or new potatoes

50 g/2 oz butter
4 tablespoons honey

Cook the small onions or new potatoes in boiling salted

water until just tender. Drain. Melt the butter in a pan and add the honey. When blended, add the onions or potatoes and cook slowly until browned and well glazed.

* * *

TO CHOOSE AND COOK SWEETCORN

Buy plump, round corn cobs which are covered in a sheath of fresh-looking green leaves. The 'tassel' which grows out of the top should be black and dead and the kernels should be yellow but not wrinkled. Before cooking, cut off the stalk and strip off the green leaves and fine silk. Place in boiling water for 5 minutes and serve piping hot with salt and melted butter.

YUM YUM YAM
Cooking time 20 minutes
SERVES 4

1 yam   juice of ½ lemon
1 tablespoon vinegar

Peel the yam and cut into chunks. Place in a bowl of cold water with the vinegar to prevent discolouring. Drain and put the yam pieces into a pan, adding just enough lightly salted water to half cover and the lemon juice. Boil until just tender. Drain and serve with butter.

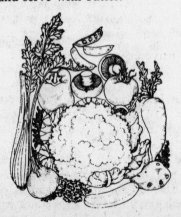

SALADS

Here is a selection of attractive salads that can be eaten as snacks, main courses or, in smaller quantities, as starters.

CRUNCHY SALAD
SERVES 4–6

2 red-skinned apples
2 teaspoons lemon juice
2 sticks of celery, chopped
225 g/8 oz cooked potato, chopped
100 g/4 oz nuts and raisins
100 g/4 oz Cheddar cheese, cubed
1 142-ml/5-fl oz carton natural yogurt
1 tablespoon salad cream

Core and dice the apples, put in a basin and toss in lemon juice to prevent discolouration. Add the celery, potato, nuts, raisins and cheese. Combine the yogurt and salad cream and add to the salad ingredients. Toss well together and chill for 1 hour before serving. This salad is good to take on picnics or for a packed lunch.

TIVOLI EGG SALAD
Cooking time 8 minutes
SERVES 4

8 eggs
150 ml/¼ pint mayonnaise
3–4 tablespoons soured cream
2 teaspoons Worcestershire sauce
½ teaspoon made mustard
salt and pepper
4 sticks of celery, chopped
paprika
½ 298-g/10½-oz can mandarin orange segments, drained
2 tomatoes, thinly sliced
lettuce and watercress to garnish

Hard-boil the eggs, cool quickly under running cold water and remove the shells. Cut the eggs in half lengthwise and scoop out the yolks into a bowl. Trim a little egg white from the egg to allow the side of each half to stand firm. Add the egg white trimmings to yolks.

Mix the mayonnaise with the soured cream, Worcestershire sauce, mustard and seasoning. Mash the egg yolks well and moisten with some of the mayonnaise mixture. Spoon or pipe into the egg white halves and arrange them in two rows on an attractive serving dish.

Mix the celery into the rest of the mayonnaise mixture and spoon over the eggs. Sprinkle the tops with paprika. Place the orange segments and tomato slices alternately in overlapping lines between the eggs and garnish with finely shredded lettuce and watercress sprigs.

CUCUMBER AND MINT SALAD

Cucumber contains a lot of water, therefore it is best to salt and drain before using.

SERVES 6

1 cucumber	1 tablespoon castor sugar
salt	1 tablespoon chopped fresh
1 onion, grated	mint
1 teaspoon dill seeds	
6 tablespoons French dressing	

Slice the cucumber thinly, with or without the peel. Place in a colander and sprinkle generously with salt. Leave to drain for 30 minutes, then rinse off the excess salt before using.

Place the cucumber in a shallow dish with the grated onion and dill seeds. Mix the French dressing with the castor sugar and mint. Spoon this dressing over cucumber.

CELERIAC AND ORANGE SALAD
Cooking time 3 minutes
SERVES 4

1 small head of celeriac	2 oranges
little lemon juice	watercress sprigs to garnish
2 tablespoons salad dressing	

Finely shred the celeriac. Put in a saucepan with enough water to cover and a little lemon juice. Bring to boil and simmer for 3 minutes. Drain. While the celeriac is still warm, toss in the salad dressing to moisten. Add the grated rind of one orange and the peeled segments of both oranges. Turn into a serving bowl and garnish with small sprigs of watercress.

POTATO SALAD
Cooking time about 15 minutes
SERVES 4–6

450 g/1 lb potatoes

150 ml/¼ pint mayonnaise
   or salad cream

salt and pepper

Boil the unpeeled potatoes in salted water until just cooked. Drain, remove the skins and dice. Mix carefully with the mayonnaise or salad cream, while the potatoes are still warm. Season.

Add any of the following to the basic mixture

Chopped parsley, onion, shallot, chives or spring onion – or any combination of these.

Chopped sweet or sour pickle, relish or chutney.

Chopped hard-boiled egg and chives.

Small cubes of cheese, chopped gherkin and a little chopped parsley.

Cottage cheese with chopped chives or chopped onion.

Diced radish, celery and unpeeled red apple.

Grated raw carrot and sultanas.

Sliced or chopped skinned tomatoes with chopped spring onion.

Chopped green or red peppers with a little chopped onion.

Cooked peas and slices of cooked small carrots.

HOT POTATO SALAD
Cooking time 15–20 minutes
SERVES 4–6

450 g/1 lb potatoes
4 tablespoons relish or
chutney

4 tablespoons salad cream
1 tablespoon vinegar
salt to taste

Boil the unpeeled potatoes in salted water until just cooked.
Drain, remove the skins and dice. Put all the ingredients into
a saucepan and warm through gently. Serve with a salad or
hot vegetarian sausages.

SWEET AND SOUR SALAD
Cooking time 15 minutes
SERVES 4–6

450 g/1 lb potatoes
½ onion, finely chopped
100 g/4 oz broad beans,
cooked
2 teaspoons French mustard

1 tablespoon sugar
pinch salt
1 142-ml/5-fl oz carton
natural yogurt
chopped fresh parsley

Boil the unpeeled potatoes in salted water until just cooked.
Drain, remove the skins and dice. Mix the potatoes, onion
and beans together. Add the mustard, sugar and salt to the
yogurt and stir well. Pour over the vegetables and mix well.
Garnish with the chopped parsley. Serve chilled.

ALFALFA SALAD TOSS

225 g/8 oz celery, finely
chopped
100 g/4 oz currants
2 carrots, grated

50 g/2 oz alfalfa sprouts (see
sprouting section page
134).

Mix the ingredients thoroughly and chill. Serve on individual
salad plates topped with a yogurt dressing (see page 125).

FRESH MUSHROOM MIX
SERVES 4

100 g/4 oz mushrooms,
  sliced
1 small potato, cooked and
  thinly sliced

50 g/2 oz bean sprouts
100 g/4 oz alfalfa sprouts
50 g/2 oz fresh peas
sesame dressing

Mix all the ingredients, except the dressing, in a large bowl
and chill until ready to serve. Toss in the sesame dressing or
any oil–based dressing just before serving.

SLIMMERS' MAYONNAISE
SERVES 1–2

2 hard–boiled egg yolks
1 tablespoon vinegar or
  lemon juice
salt and pepper

¼ teaspoon dry mustard
1–2 tablespoons fat-free
  yogurt

Mash the egg yolks until smooth. Mix in the vinegar and
seasonings. Stir in enough yogurt to make a mayonnaise
consistency.

You can flavour this mayonnaise with any of the following:
finely chopped garlic, capers, gherkins, parsley, chervil,
chives, green pepper, watercress, finely grated onion, chilli
sauce, paprika or cayenne pepper.

COUNTRY EGG SALAD
SERVES 4

8 hard–boiled eggs
shredded lettuce leaves
1 10-cm/4-inch piece
  cucumber, cut in strips
4 sticks of celery, thinly
  sliced

1 medium carrot, finely
  grated
75 g/3 oz grapes, de-seeded
  and quartered
salt and pepper
about 2 tablespoons vinegar

Quarter the eggs. Arrange the lettuce round the edge of a

serving dish. Mix the remaining ingredients together, except the egg quarters. Pile the mixture on to the dish and attractively arrange the eggs on top.

GRAPEFRUIT AND CHEESE TUMBLE
SERVES 2 or 4

1 lettuce
225 g/8 oz Lancashire cheese, crumbled
1 grapefruit, skinned and segmented
2 sticks of celery, chopped
2 spring onions or few chives finely chopped
150 ml/¼ pint natural yogurt
paprika to garnish

Arrange the lettuce in a serving dish. Mix all the other ingredients together and pile on the lettuce. Serve sprinkled with the paprika.

PASTA AND CHEESE SALAD
SERVES 4

350 g/12 oz short macaroni, cooked
2 onions, finely chopped
450 g/1 lb tomatoes, skinned and chopped
3 sticks of celery, chopped
275 g/10 oz cheese, cubed
150 ml/¼ pint soured cream
2 tablespoons mayonnaise
salt and pepper
sprigs of parsley to garnish

Carefully toss all the ingredients together in a serving bowl, adding salt and pepper to taste. Garnish with the parsley sprigs.

VARIETY VEGETABLE SALAD
Cooking time about 15 minutes
SERVES 4–6

450 g/1 lb small potatoes
1 cauliflower, broken into
  florets
3 carrots, cut into thin strips
4 sticks celery, diced
100 g/4 oz whole green
  beans

100 g/4 oz garden peas
150 ml/¼ pint mayonnaise
150 ml/¼ pint soured cream
chopped chives to garnish

Boil the potatoes until just cooked. Cook the cauliflower, carrots, celery, beans and peas for 2–3 minutes only. Combine the mayonnaise and soured cream and coat the vegetables while still warm. Sprinkle with chives.

WALDORF MACARONI SALAD
Cooking time about 10 minutes
SERVES 4

5 oz wholewheat short cut
  macaroni
4 red-skinned apples, sliced
  and chopped
2 tablespoons lemon juice
4 sticks of celery, chopped

3 tablespoons raisins
salt and pepper
150–300 ml/¼–½ pint salad
  cream
4 tablespoons walnuts

Cook the macaroni in boiling salted water for about 10 minutes. Drain and rinse under cold running water until completely cold. Mix the macaroni with the remaining ingredients and blend them well together. Chill before serving.

PASTA SLAW
Cooking time about 10 minutes
SERVES 4–6

175 g/6 oz short cut macaroni
275 g/10 oz white cabbage, shredded
2 sticks of celery, chopped
2 medium carrots, grated

1 small onion, diced
for the dressing
300 ml/½ pint salad cream
2 tablespoons vinegar
1 tablespoon sugar
salt and pepper

Bring a large pan of salted water to the boil, add the macaroni and simmer for about 10 minutes. Drain and rinse under cold running water until cold. Place in a large bowl and add all the remaining ingredients. Stir together the dressing ingredients and spoon over the pasta slaw. Mix well and leave to chill.

FLORIDA FRUITY
SERVES 4

2 large thick-skinned oranges
2 dessert apples, grated
100 g/4 oz cottage cheese
1 142-ml/5-fl oz carton natural yogurt

1 stick of celery, finely chopped
¼ teaspoon cinnamon
2 pineapple rings or apple slices to decorate

Cut the oranges in half. Scoop out the centres, reserving the orange flesh and juice. Mix the orange flesh, apple, cottage cheese, yogurt, celery and cinnamon together. Divide the mixture between the orange cups. Decorate each with half a pineapple ring or slice of apple.

SMOKY SALAD
SERVES 2

1 small crisp lettuce
1 carrot cut into strips
6 spring onions
2 tomatoes, quartered
1 crispy apple (such as
Granny Smith), cut into
small chunks
1 handful roasted sunflower
seeds
1 small bunch watercress
3 sticks celery chopped into
½-inch strips
100 g/4 oz smoked cheese
(such as Applewood or
Bavarian smoked), cut
into cubes
2 tablespoons chopped
chives
2 tablespoons chopped mint
leaves
for the dressing
4 tablespoons oil (corn or
olive)
2 tablespoons lemon juice
¼ teaspoon made mustard
1 clove garlic, chopped
finely
salt and black pepper

Place all the dressing ingredients into a small dressing bottle
and shake well. Put to chill a little in the fridge for about 30
minutes.

Shred the lettuce and arrange at the bottom of a salad bowl.
Toss together the rest of the ingredients with the dressing
and spoon over the lettuce.

This dish can be served as a side-salad with an omelette or
as a main salad with a jacket potato. If smoked cheese is not
to your taste, use Gouda instead.

COTTAGE CHEESE NUT SALAD
SERVES 3

350 g/12 oz cottage cheese
4 tablespoons chopped
pineapple
25 g/1 oz chopped hazelnuts
1 crisp apple, diced small

Mix all the ingredients together and chill slightly. Serve on
a bed of lettuce surrounded by tomato and cucumber slices.

SPROUTING DISHES

Are you the world's worst when it comes to growing greenery? Is gardening something you just don't dig? Then how would you like to grow your own supply of all-the-year-round fresh vegetables with almost no effort at all?

You don't even need a garden – all you need is a glass jar, a small piece of cheesecloth and a rubber band, to grow tasty, healthy food packed with proteins, vitamins and minerals.

Can you imagine a vegetable that is ready to eat in 3–6 days; that does not need soil or sunlight and needs hardly any attention?

I'm talking about *sprouting seeds* – an unusual and delicious addition to anyone's diet. They can be eaten on their own, in salads or sandwiches, cooked, or blended with a practically unlimited range of foods. There are now a wide range of sprouting seeds available and I recommend them for their goodness and their fresh crunchy taste. You really only need to sprout a little at a time as the seeds yield up to ten times their own weight in a matter of days.

Thompson and Morgan provide a varied selection of organically grown sprouting seeds which can be obtained by post or at some garden centres. So do most health food shops.

HOW TO SPROUT

You can if you wish buy specially designed seed-sprouters for a few pounds, but the cheapest and simplest method is the jam, fruit or coffee jar method.

1 All you do is spoon a small quantity of seed – say, 2 level teaspoons – into the glass jar. Place a piece of muslin, cheesecloth (or even a piece cut out of a pair of tights) over the top of the jar and secure firmly with a rubber band.

2 Fill with tepid water, shake thoroughly and drain. Repeat a couple of times, then leave the jar on its side to drain.

3 Repeat the process of filling with tepid water, shaking and draining twice daily until the sprouts are ready for eating – which should be in 3–6 days, depending on the seed.

And that's all there is to it.

You can keep the sprouted seeds in the storage compartment of your refrigerator if you wish at approximately 1°C (34°F) in sealed polythene bags. They should keep for 3 weeks in excellent condition with no loss of flavour or crispness.

Do's and Don'ts
All you have to remember is:
Don't lay the jar on a radiator or anything else producing considerable heat;
Don't rinse with very hot water;
Do discard any seeds that haven't sprouted after 6 days;
If the seed sprouts smell slightly less than fresh, then do step up the rinsing or grow under cooler conditions.

Some Seeds to Try

Sandwich Mix Sprouts: produce a blend of sweet and sour flavours. They combine well with cheese, tomato, TVP beefburgers and pickles. They are high in the Vitamins A and B complex group, too.

Spicy Fenugreek: which, at the first sign of sprouting has the aroma and a hint of the flavour of curry. But as the sprout grows to about 1 cm/½ inch, the curry smell vanishes. Fenugreek has long been believed to possess healing qualities which aid in the treatment of gastric and other intestinal disorders, including ulcers. It is rich in iron and Vitamin C. But here's a warning – after eating fenugreek, a strange fruity smell of curry may exude from the pores of your body!

Salad Alfalfa: a fresh green salad vegetable containing around 40 per cent protein and tasting like sweet freshly picked garden peas. Half a cupful of sprouted alfalfa after 72 hours' growing contains as much Vitamin C as six glasses of orange juice.

Soya Bean Sprouts: the highest source of protein in vegetables and providers of zinc and calcium. They need more rinsing to stay fresh than other seeds.

Alphatoco Sprouts: crisp and crunchy, sweet and full of flavour, containing good amounts of Vitamins C and E.

Adzuki Beans: sprouted for centuries by the Chinese, Manchurians, Japanese and Koreans. They have a crispy, sweet, nutty flavour.

Herbal Green Mint Sprouts: they have a clean, clear green mint flavour. Can be added to salads or lightly cooked and combined with peas, carrots and beans.

Saucy Sandwich Relish: sweet and spicy, they make a good sandwich filling and are a piquant addition to salads or a saucy ingredient for oriental recipes.

Lentil Sprouts: they have a distinctly nutty flavour, on the sweet side and can be eaten raw, in salads, steamed, made into soup or baked.

AVOCADO CUCUMBER CRUNCH

2 cucumbers	pinch salt
1 small avocado	50 g/2 oz alfalfa sprouts,
1 tablespoon lemon juice	chopped
1 onion, finely chopped	6 cherry tomatoes, thinly
dash of tobasco pepper sauce	sliced

Cut the unpeeled cucumbers diagonally across in 1-cm/½-inch slices. Drain on an absorbent kitchen paper. Mash the avocado flesh with a fork and whip until creamy. Add the lemon juice, onion, tabasco, salt and sprouts. Mix well, then spread the cucumber slices with the avocado mixture and top each with a slice of tomato.

CHEWY CHEESE SANDWICH
Cooking time 10–15 minutes
Oven temperature Moderate 180°C, 350°F, Gas Mark 4
SERVES 4

4 slices wholewheat bread	2 eggs
250 ml/8 fl oz white wine	50 g/2 oz alfalfa sprouts
100 g/4 oz Cheddar cheese,	40 g/1½ oz butter
grated	

Place the bread on a greased baking sheet and sprinkle the wine over. Beat the cheese, eggs and sprouts together and spread on the bread slices. Dot with butter and bake in a moderate oven for 10–15 minutes until puffy.

CURRIED FENUGREEK
Cooking time 15 minutes
SERVES 4

1 small onion, chopped
2 tablespoons oil
2 teaspoons curry powder
100 g/4 oz fenugreek
  sprouts, chopped

1 teaspoon cornflour
3 tablespoons warm water

Fry the onion in the oil in a frying pan until transparent. Add the curry powder and fenugreek sprouts, and mix well. Blend the cornflour with the warm water and add to the sprouts. Cook, stirring, until the mixture thickens.

POTATOES AND FENUGREEK
Cooking time 10 minutes
SERVES 4

450 g/1 lb potatoes, boiled in
  their jackets
2 tablespoons oil
½ teaspoon turmeric

100 g/4 oz fenugreek sprouts
pinch cayenne pepper
1 teaspoon salt

Peel and chop the boiled potatoes. Heat the oil in a large frying pan, add the potatoes and turmeric. Sauté for 3 minutes, stirring constantly. Add the fenugreek sprouts, cayenne pepper and salt. Mix well and continue cooking, covered, for 5 minutes.

ALFALFA SPROUT RAREBIT
Cooking time 10 minutes
SERVES 4

450 ml/¾ pint water
150–175 g/5–6 oz cashew
  nuts
1 teaspoon salt
1 tablespoon flour
1 tablespoon minced dried
  onion or 1 tablespoon
  minced fresh
3 tablespoons cornflour

15 g/½ oz butter
3 tablespoons tahini (sesame
  paste) or raw nut butter
1 tablespoon chopped chives
25 g/1 oz stoned olives,
  sliced
75 g/3 oz alfalfa sprouts
pimentos and ripe olives to
  garnish

Place the water, cashews, salt, flour, onion and cornflour in a liquidiser and blend for 30 seconds. Pour into a pan over a low heat, stirring until the sauce thickens. Remove from the heat and add the butter, tahini, chives, olives and alfalfa sprouts. Mix well and reheat but do not boil. Serve on whole-wheat toast and garnish with strips of pimento and ripe olives.

DUTTY'S CRUNCHY BUTTY

1 small French loaf
butter or margarine to
  spread
sandwich mix sprouts
alphatoco sprouts

alfalfa sprouts
Cheddar cheese spread
several sticks of celery
salt and pepper

Split the French loaf, or similar loaf, with a knife and butter it inside. Spread liberally with the Cheddar cheese spread (or any cheese spread) and cover with handfuls of selected sprouts. Chop the celery into 1-cm/½-inch chunks and spread on top of sprouts. Season well, close the loaf together and slice into man-size chunks. A really refreshing munch for home, party or picnic.

SIAMESE FRIED RICE
Cooking time about 20 minutes
SERVES 4–6

2 tablespoons oil
225 g/8 oz onion, chopped
12 oz cooked rice
2 eggs, beaten with 2
   tablespoons soy sauce

50 g/2 oz salad sprouts,
   steamed
salt and pepper

Heat the oil in a large frying pan or wok, add the onion and fry until golden. Stir in the rice and sauté for 3 minutes. Add the egg mixture, turning it into the rice. Do not keep stirring as the rice will become sticky. Add the salad sprouts and seasoning, turning carefully once or twice. Serve when heated through.

   A spicy relish such as chutney goes well with this dish, plus cucumber sambal (see page 122) and a fruit dessert.

COTTAGE CHEESE DIP

225 g/8 oz cottage cheese
1 clove garlic, crushed
¼ teaspoon caraway seeds
4 tablespoons natural yogurt

25 g/1 oz fenugreek sprouts,
   finely chopped
salt

Press the cottage cheese through a sieve and add the remaining ingredients, mixing well. Chill for 2 hours. Serve with crusty French bread, carrot or celery sticks.

SWISS EGGS
SERVES 3 or 6

6 hard-boiled eggs
25 g/1 oz soft butter
25 g/1 oz Swiss cheese,
   grated

25 g/1 oz alfalfa sprouts
paprika to garnish

Cut the eggs in half lengthwise. Scoop out the yolks and

cream with the butter and grated cheese. Add the alfalfa sprouts and mix well. Spoon into the egg white halves. Garnish with paprika or a sprinkle of sprouts.

So there we are – sprouting for beginners. It may sound weird and something you've never thought of doing, but that's what vegetarianism is – or should be – all about. Experimentation can lead to more pleasurable and healthier eating habits. In other words, don't knock it until you've tried it. So come on – start sprouting with health!

Egg Dishes

If vegetarians include eggs and dairy produce in their diet, they are what's known as ovo-lacto vegetarians. Some vegetarians refuse to eat eggs because of the battery egg production and because of the difficulty of finding outlets where free range eggs may be obtained. (Free range eggs have a higher nutritive value.) However, there now exists a society – FREGG (The Free Range Egg Society), 37 Tanza Road, London NW3) – which will provide you with a list of recommended farms and shops providing free range eggs, on receipt of an SAE.

Eggs are a good source of protein, iron, calcium, and Vitamins A, Bs, D and E. They are also light in calories – the average egg contains about 80–90 calories. Unfortunately, eggs also have a high cholesterol content and some nutritionists recommend people to limit themselves to three a week. So once again the choice is with the individual. I eat free range eggs, but not too many.

Here are some cracking ideas for egg dishes:

OMELETTES

'Omelette' is a dirty word to most vegetarians. Just the mere mention of it is enough to send them into a fit. The reason is that quite often an omelette is the best that unimaginative restaurateurs and hotel owners can dish up, when faced with someone who doesn't partake of meat.

Very often the 'omelette' is poorly cooked, resembling a dried pancake folded in half with charred remains of mushrooms or stringy cheese sitting in the middle. The best remedy is not to go to those places, but to get yourself a decent omelette pan and have a go yourself. The omelette pan, made of cast-iron or aluminium, should be about 5 cm/ 2 inches deep with a thick base and curved sides. These days, you can even buy an omelette pan which actually folds in the middle for bringing the two halves together!

To make a successful omelette:
Use the right size of pan. Use a 15-cm/6-inch pan for omelettes made with two size 1 or 2 (large) eggs or two or three size 3 or 4 (standard) eggs. Use a 7-inch pan for omelettes made with three size 1 or 2 (large) or three or four size 3 or 4 (standard) eggs. Always allow at least 2 eggs per person and 1 teaspoon of cold water for each egg used.
Cook omelettes in butter.
Cook them as quickly as possible.
Serve immediately the omelette is cooked.

THE FRENCH OMELETTE
(Basic recipe)
Cooking time about 5 minutes

SERVES 1

3 size 3 or 4 (standard) eggs   salt and pepper
3 teaspoons cold water   15 g/½ oz butter

Break the eggs into a basin, add the water and seasoning. Beat lightly with a fork, just enough to break up the eggs. Melt the butter in an omelette pan, turn up the heat and, when the butter is sizzling, but not brown, pour in the omelette mixture. With a fork or palette knife (use a wooden one for non-stick pans), draw the mixture from the sides to the middle of the pan, allowing the uncooked egg to set quickly. Repeat until all the runny egg is lightly cooked, about 5 minutes. When the top is still slightly runny, fold over one third of the omelette lifting away from the handle of the pan. Remove from heat.

To turn out on to a *warm* plate, hold the handle of the pan with the palm uppermost. Shake the omelette to the edge of the pan and tip the pan over, so making another fold.

Add to the uncooked mixture one of the following:
* 1 tablespoon chopped fresh parsley
* 1 tablespoon chopped fresh chives
* 1 tablespoon chopped spring onion tops
* 50 g/2 oz cooked pasta and 1 tablespoon spring onion tops
* 50 g/2 oz finely grated cheese

* *For the classical Omelette aux fines herbes*, add 1½ tablespoons chopped mixed fresh parsley, chives, tarragon and chervil

* *For a tasty uncooked filling*, add along the line of the first fold of the cooked omelette 25 g/1 oz cream cheese mixed with 1 tablespoon chopped chives or watercress, some shredded lettuce and 1 tablespoon single cream

* *For fillings pre-cooked in a little butter*, add one of the following:
* 100 g/4 oz cooked sliced potato, fried until crisp, with herbs added to the complete mixture
* 2 tablespoons croûtons, fried with crushed clove garlic until golden and crisp
* 50 g/2 oz asparagus tips
* 75 g/3 oz sliced aubergines, salted and rinsed before cooking
* 50 g/2 oz skinned chopped tomato, sprinkled with a pinch of oregano

For a Swiss Mountain Omelette filling mix 50 g/2 oz finely grated Cheddar cheese with 2 tablespoons double cream. Place half of the mixture in the omelette before folding and the remaining mixture on top. Place under a hot grill for a few moments until the topping is bubbling and golden.

EL CID'S SUPREMO SPANISH OMELETTE
Cooking time 15–20 minutes
SERVES 1

1 tablespoon olive oil	3 size 3 or 4 (standard) eggs
100 g/4 oz onion, chopped	3 teaspoons cold water
175 g/6 oz cooked potato, diced	salt and pepper

Heat the oil in the omelette pan, add the onion and cook slowly until soft. Add the diced potato and heat through. Meanwhile, prepare the omelette mixture as for the French omelette (see page 142).

When the onion mixture is hot, pour in the egg and cook

143

until the underside is firm and the top runny. Place the pan under a hot grill for about 30 seconds or until the top is just set. Don't fold the omelette – slide it out flat on to a warmed serving plate.

Chopped green or red peppers may be added with the onion.

FRIED EGGS

'So what's new about fried eggs?' I hear you cry. Here are two recipes that raise fried eggs to the standard of 'haute cuisine'.

EGGS CHOU-FLEUR
Cooking time 40 minutes
SERVES 4

1 medium cauliflower or 350 g/12 oz courgettes	100 g/4 oz mushrooms or 1 227-g/8-oz can sweetcorn, drained
2 tablespoons oil	salt and pepper
25 g/1 oz butter	4 eggs
1 clove garlic, crushed	550 g/2 oz cheese, grated
4 tomatoes	

Break the cauliflower into small sprigs or trim and chop the courgettes. Heat the oil and butter in a large frying pan, and add the cauliflower or courgettes and garlic. Fry gently for about 25 minutes until almost tender. Chop the tomatoes and mushrooms, add to the pan with seasoning and cook for 5–10 minutes. Make four spaces in the mixture and break an egg into each space. Sprinkle with the cheese. Cook for 3–5 minutes to set the eggs. Serve hot with crisp bread rolls.

EGGS JOCKEY
Cooking time 30 minutes
SERVES 4

1 447-g/15¾-oz can peas or
   1 340-g/12-oz packet
   frozen
100 g/4 oz mushrooms
65 g/2½ oz butter
salt and pepper

lemon juice or vinegar
4 1-cm/½-inch thick slices
   of bread, cut in 10-cm/4-
   inch rounds
1 can Tartex pâté
4 eggs

Heat the canned peas in their juice or cook the frozen peas in salted water, then drain. Slice the mushrooms thinly and put into a pan with 15 g/½ oz of the butter. Sprinkle with seasoning and lemon juice or vinegar and cook for 2–3 minutes. Reserving a few slices of mushroom, mix the remainder with the peas and keep hot.

Heat the remaining butter in a frying pan and fry the bread on both sides until crisp. Drain and spread each round with the pâté. Place on heated serving dish and keep hot.

Fry the eggs in the same pan, drain and serve on the bread. Spread the peas round the bread and top each egg with mushroom slices. Keep hot. Heat the butter left in the pan, add seasoning and a squeeze of lemon juice. When it's nicely browned, pour over each egg and serve.

BOILED EGGS

Keep eggs at room temperature for a while before cooking as eggs straight from the refrigerator have a tendency to crack. If an egg does develop a crack after placing in water, a little vinegar or a pinch of salt will help to harden the escaping white and close the crack.

To boil, place the egg carefully into a pan, cover completely with cold water. Bring to boiling point, then reduce the heat to simmering and time from this moment:

★ Soft boiled – from 3 minutes for size 1 or 2 (large) eggs to 2¼ minutes for size 5 or 6 (small)

★ Hard white, soft yolk – from 4½ minutes for size 1 or 2 (large) eggs to 3 minutes for size 5 or 6 (small)

* Hard-boiled – from 8 minutes for size 1 or 2 (large) eggs to 6 minutes for size 5 or 6 (small)

To coddle eggs, place the eggs carefully into a pan of boiling water (off the heat), covering them completely. Put the lid back on the pan and time from this moment. Cooking time ranges from 6½ minutes for size 5 or 6 (small) eggs to 8 or 9 minutes for size 1 or 2 (large) ones.

BRETON EGGS
Cooking time about 25 minutes
SERVES 4

8 eggs
50 g/2 oz butter
675 g/1½ lb onions, sliced
  thinly
150 ml/¼ pint stock
salt and pepper

8 ½ inch thick rounds
  French bread
25 g/1 oz butter
3 teaspoons French mustard
chopped fresh parsley to
  garnish

Coddle or soft boil the eggs (see page 145) and remove the shells. Keep the eggs in warm water. Melt the butter in a frying pan and fry the onions until tender, allowing them to brown all over. Stir in the stock and seasoning, and bring to the boil. Spoon into a shallow dish and keep hot.

Spread the bread on one side with some of the butter and the mustard. Place under a heated grill until crisp. Arrange the bread, buttered side upwards, on the onions. Dry the eggs and place on the bread rounds. Dot the eggs with butter and grill for 1–2 minutes. Serve hot sprinkled with chopped parsley.

CURRIED EGGS
Cooking time 50 minutes
SERVES 4

8 eggs
2 large onions, thinly sliced
1 tablespoon oil
3 tablespoons curry powder
   to taste
1 tablespoon flour
1 large cooking apple
600 ml/1 pint stock
1 tablespoon chutney

juice of ½ lemon
1 tablespoon apricot jam
1 tablespoon soft brown
   sugar
pinch salt
4 tablespoons cream
225 g/8 oz long-grain rice to
   serve

Hard-boil the eggs (see page 145), remove the shells and keep the eggs in warm water. Fry the onion gently in the oil for 10 minutes until tender, but not coloured. Stir in the curry powder and flour, and continue cooking for 2–3 minutes. Peel, core and chop the apple, add to the pan and cook for 3 minutes. Gradually pour in the stock and stir until boiling, then add the chutney, lemon juice, jam, sugar and salt. Simmer, stirring occasionally, for 25–30 minutes. Strain the sauce, return to the saucepan with the cream and reheat without boiling.

Spoon the boiled rice into a heated serving dish, arrange the eggs on top and pour the curry sauce over. Serve with poppadums.

SCRAMBLED EGGS

Points to remember
* Use a thick pan and a gentle heat.
* Stir all the time – never leaving the eggs.
* Remove from the heat just before the eggs are fully set as they continue cooking in their own heat.

Cooking time 3 minutes
SERVES 2

4 eggs
salt and pepper

25 g/1 oz butter
1 tablespoon single cream

Beat the eggs, salt and pepper together. Melt the butter in a thick pan and pour in the eggs. Stir all the time over a low heat until the eggs are soft and creamy. Remove from the heat and add the cream. This will stop further cooking and add to the flavour.

Serving suggestions: You can serve scrambled eggs *on* buttered toast, fried bread or savoury biscuits.

Or scrambled eggs can be served *in* sandwiches, rolls, baked potatoes, cooked mushroom caps, cooked tomato cups, vol-au-vent cases, pastry boats and pastry cases, large and small.

Now for two scrumptious scrambles . . .

BUBBLYATA
Cooking time 8 minutes
SERVES 4

3 tomatoes, skinned
25 g/1 oz butter
8 eggs
salt and pepper

2 tablespoons cooked peas
2 teaspoons chopped chives
  or spring onion tops
1 tablespoon single cream

Chop the tomatoes roughly and cook in the butter for 2–3 minutes. Beat the eggs lightly with the salt and pepper, and add the cooked peas and chives or spring onion tops. Pour the egg mixture on to the tomatoes and cook as in the basic recipe, adding the cream at the end. Serve on toast.

LEMON AND PARSLEY SCRAMBLE
Cooking time about 12 minutes
SERVES 4

50 g/2 oz butter
2 medium onions, finely
  chopped
8 eggs
2 tablespoons chopped fresh
  parsley

grated rind of ½ lemon
salt and pepper
1 tablespoon cream

Melt the butter, add the onion and cook gently without browning. Beat the eggs with the chopped parsley, grated lemon rind, salt and pepper. Pour into the pan and cook as the basic recipe, adding the cream at the end.

POACHED EGGS

To cook, break the egg on to a saucer. Heat 7.5 cm/3 inches water in a pan. Swirl the water round and carefully slide the egg into the 'whirlpool'; this will keep the egg in a round shape. Simmer until ready – about 4 minutes, lift out on a perforated spoon and 'blot' on a clean folded cloth or absorbent kitchen paper and serve.

POACHED EGGS FLORENTINE
Cooking time about 30 minutes
Oven temperature Hot 220°C, 425°F, Gas Mark 7
SERVES 4

1 kg/2 lb fresh spinach or about 450 g/1 lb frozen
salt
65 g/2½ oz butter
40 g/1½ oz flour

450 ml/¾ pint milk
75 g/3 oz cheese, grated
½ teaspoon made mustard
pinch cayenne pepper
8 eggs

Cook the spinach in very little water, then drain thoroughly and chop. Mix in 15 g/½ oz of the butter, with salt to taste, and spread in a buttered flameproof dish.

Melt 40 g/1½ oz of the butter, mix in the flour and gradually stir in the milk. Stir over a low heat for 2–3 minutes until thickened and cooked. Add 50 g/2 oz of the cheese, salt, mustard and cayenne pepper. Poach the eggs and arrange on the spinach. Cover with the sauce, sprinkle with the rest of the cheese and dot with the remaining butter. Place under a heated grill or in a hot oven to melt and brown the cheese.

CRECY EGGS
Cooking time 35 minutes
SERVES 4

450 g/1 lb carrots
1 small onion
1–2 sticks of celery
600 ml/1 pint stock

salt and pepper
8 eggs
chopped fresh parsley

Mince or grate the carrots, onion and celery. Put in a saucepan with the stock and seasoning. Cover and simmer for about 30 minutes until soft.

Spread the mixture into a heated serving dish. Poach the eggs then 'blot' them (see page 149). Arrange on top of the vegetables and sprinkle with parsley.

POACHED EGGS FOR SALADS

Cook the eggs for 4 minutes and slide immediately into cold water, to keep the whites moist and the egg yolk soft. Lift out the eggs when needed, using a perforated spoon. Dry them on a clean folded cloth or absorbent kitchen paper, then trim the whites with a pastry cutter.

Coat with mayonnaise and arrange on a serving dish with various salad ingredients or surround with decoratively cut cooked vegetables.

SOUFFLÉS

Many people seem to be scared of attempting to make a soufflé, fearing they'll end up with something resembling a chef's hat that someone's just sat on! The people who know best – the British Egg Information Service – say there are only six steps to successful soufflés, and this is what they recommend:

1 *The white sauce mixture* Melt 75 g/3 oz butter in a thickish pan over a low heat. As it melts, stir in 50 g/2 oz sifted plain flour. Slowly add 300 ml/½ pint milk, stirring to keep the mixture smooth. (This is easier to do with warmed milk.) Bring the mixture to boiling point, stirring all the time. Cook

for 3 minutes, still stirring. And there you have the basic soufflé mixture.

Note: For savoury soufflés, always season the basic white sauce with salt and pepper. For sweet soufflés, always sweeten the basic white sauce with 50 g/2 oz castor sugar.

2 *Add your filling now* Add the filling to the basic soufflé mixture before you add the eggs (see soufflé fillings).

3 *Add your eggs this way* You will need 3 size 1 or 2 (large) eggs. The yolks must be separated from the whites. Beat the yolks very thoroughly and mix in with the white sauce and filling. Beat the whites until they are so stiff that they stay in the basin when you turn it upside-down. Fold these gently, but thoroughly, into the mixture.

4 *Prepare your soufflé dish this way* Use a 1-litre/2-pint (minimum) soufflé dish – this is important. Grease it well (olive oil is best).

5 *Cook your soufflé this way* Fill the prepared soufflé dish and cook on the middle shelf in a moderately hot oven (190°C, 375°F, Mark 5) for about 45 minutes. Cooking heat and timing is very important.

6 *THE SOUFFLE MUST BE EATEN AT ONCE.*

SOUFFLE FILLINGS

Here are some suggested fillings for soufflés.

* 100 g/4 oz grated Cheddar cheese and ½ teaspoon dry mustard.
* 175g/6 oz cooked fresh or canned asparagus, finely chopped.
* About 225 g/8 oz cooked mashed aubergine and 50 g/2 oz chopped sautéed mushrooms flavoured with garlic.
* 4 tablespoons tomato purée.
* 4 tablespoons thick, sweet apple purée, flavoured with a little lemon juice.
* 4 tablespoons thick, sweet apricot purée, flavoured with a little lemon juice.
* 1½ mashed bananas, flavoured with orange and lemon juice.
* 4 tablespoons thick sweet blackberry purée.

* 175 g/6 oz chopped fresh strawberries, flavoured with a little lemon juice.
* 1 tablespoon rum. Serve the soufflé with rum sauce.
* 175 g/6 oz chopped canned mandarins, flavoured with orange juice.
* Add finely grated rind of 1 lemon and the juice of ½ lemon.
* 175 g/6 oz raspberries, flavoured with a little lemon juice.

TORTILLA
Cooking time 35 minutes
Oven temperature Moderately Hot 200°C, 400°F, Gas Mark 6
SERVES 4

100 g/4 oz green beans, sliced	8 eggs
1 medium red pepper	salt and pepper
1 small onion, thinly sliced	2 tablespoons water
	butter

Boil the green beans, pepper and onion together in a little water until they are just soft, then drain. Beat the eggs with the seasoning and water. Grease a shallow baking dish with the butter, add the vegetables and pour in the eggs. Bake in a moderately hot oven for about 20 minutes until the egg is set. Cut in wedges and serve hot with Tomatorange salad (see page 56).

Snacks, Tasties and Toasties

CELERY SCRAMBLE
Cooking time about 12 minutes
SERVES 4

1 298-g/10½-oz condensed   8 eggs
    celery soup

Warm the undiluted soup in a pan. Beat the eggs together lightly and pour into the soup. Cook as for scrambled eggs (see page 147).

POTTED CHESHIRE
Cooking time about 15 minutes
Makes 225 g/8 oz

225 g/8 oz Cheshire cheese,   few mixed dried herbs
    grated   salt and pepper
3 tablespoons beer   little melted butter
50 g/2 oz butter

Put the cheese, beer, butter, herbs, salt and pepper in a bowl over a pan of simmering water. Heat, stirring, until melted and thoroughly combined. Beat well and spoon into a serving pot. Pour a little melted butter over the top to seal.
    Chill well and serve on Cornish wafers or fingers of whole-wheat toast.

LANCASHIRE TOPPER
Cooking time 5 minutes
SERVES 1

50 g/2 oz Lancashire cheese,   dash Worcestershire sauce
    crumbled   pinch mustard
3 tablespoons milk   salt and pepper
1 teaspoon chutney

Slowly melt the crumbled Lancashire cheese in a pan with the milk, chutney, Worcestershire sauce, mustard, salt and pepper. Stir until the mixture is thick and creamy. Serve on toast or wafers.

SAVOURY POTATO CAKES
Cooking time 30 minutes
Oven temperature Moderate 180°C, 350°F, Gas Mark 4
Makes 6–7 potato cakes

1 small onion, boiled
1 kg/2 lb mashed potatoes

pinch salt or garlic salt
50 g/2 oz flour

Mix the boiled onion into the potatoes until thoroughly mashed together. Add the salt and 25 g/1 oz flour, mix well. Shape into 6–7 potato cakes on a floured surface, using the rest of the flour. Place the potato cakes on a greased baking tray and bake in a moderate oven for 30 minutes, turning after 15 minutes, until golden brown.

ASPARAGUS EGGS
Cooking time about 40 minutes

SERVES 4

1 clove garlic, crushed
1 tablespoon oil
1 tablespoon plain flour
1.15 litres/2 pints vegetable
   stock
2 tablespoons chopped fresh
   parsley

salt and pepper
50 g/2 oz cooked peas
75 g/3 oz cooked fresh or
   canned asparagus tips
4 hard-boiled eggs

Fry the garlic in the oil until it starts to brown. Stir in the flour and gradually add the stock and parsley. Season with salt and pepper and allow to simmer until reduced by half. Add the peas and asparagus, and heat through over a low heat for 10 minutes. Halve the hard-boiled eggs lengthwise and arrange in a heated serving dish. Pour the mixture over and serve with new potatoes.

CHEVREUSE EGGS
Cooking time about 25 minutes
Oven temperature Moderate 180°C, 350°F, Gas Mark 4
SERVES 4

450 g/1 lb fresh, canned or
    frozen green beans
50 g/2 oz butter
8 eggs

50 g/2 oz cheese, grated
15 g/½ oz white
    breadcrumbs

Cook the beans, or heat and drain the canned ones. Grease
a large ovenproof dish with most of the butter. Heat the dish
and add the beans. Break the eggs on top, sprinkle with the
cheese and breadcrumbs and dot with the remaining butter.
Bake in a moderate oven for 10–15 minutes and serve hot
with duchesse potatoes (see page 112).

QUICK PIZZAS
Cooking time about 10 minutes
SERVES 2 or 4

4 crumpets
butter
4 tomatoes, skinned and
    sliced

175 g/6 oz Cheddar cheese,
    sliced
salt and pepper

Grill the crumpets on the underside until browned. Turn
them over, toast till slightly browned, then butter and cover
with sliced tomatoes and seasoning. Top with the slices of
cheese and grill gently until the cheese begins to melt.

POTATO CHEESE CRISPS
Cooking time about 8 minutes
SERVES 2–4

1 large potato
25 g/1 oz self-raising flour
50 g/2 oz cheese, grated

1 egg, beaten
salt and pepper
oil for shallow frying

Grate the raw potato finely and pour off the liquid. Mix with the flour, cheese and egg, adding salt and pepper to taste. Fry spoonfuls of the mixture in hot oil, browning on both sides. Drain on absorbent kitchen paper and serve hot.

Curried baked beans Liven up canned baked beans by adding curry powder to them, to whatever strength the roof of your mouth can stand. Serve hot on slices of toast.

QUICK POTATO OMELETTE
Cooking time about 12 minutes
SERVES 1

1 (leftover) boiled potato,   2 eggs
   diced   salt and pepper
25 g/1 oz butter

Fry the diced potato in the melted butter until slightly brown. Beat the eggs, adding the salt and pepper, then pour over the potato. Cook as for an omelette (see page 141), making sure the potato is evenly distributed.

If liked, a little chopped onion may be added to the potato or grated cheese to the eggs.

BUBBLY CHEESE 'N' ONION
Cooking time 20 minutes
Oven temperature Moderate 180°C, 350°F, Gas Mark 4
SERVES 2

100 g/4 oz Lancashire cheese,   1 medium onion
   crumbled   2 tablespoons milk

Crumble the cheese into an ovenproof dish. Chop the onion finely. Add the onion and milk to the cheese and stir together. Bake in a moderate oven for 20 minutes until the cheese has melted. Serve spread on buttered wholewheat bread.

LENTIL SPREAD
Cooking time about 30 minutes

100 g/4 oz lentils, soaked
150 ml/¼ pint water
1 small onion
2 cloves
1 small bay leaf
25 g/1 oz butter or
  margarine

½ teaspoon fresh or dried
  mixed herbs
pinch garlic salt
salt and pepper

Thoroughly wash the lentils. Place in a small pan with the water, onion (stuck with the cloves) and bay leaf. Bring to the boil, then simmer until the lentils are soft and most of the water evaporated. Remove the onion, cloves and bay leaf. Mix the butter or margarine, herbs, garlic salt, salt and pepper into the lentils. Stir together thoroughly, then place the mixture in a basin.

Serve hot, spread on buttered toast, or allow to cool and set in the basin and use with salad or for a cold picnic spread. Any leftovers can be reheated and served hot.

YEAST EGGSTRACT SAVOURY
Cooking time 5 minutes
SERVES 1

2 eggs
½ teaspoon yeast extract
salt and pepper
1 small onion, cooked and
  chopped

1 teaspoon chopped fresh
  parsley
20 g/¾ oz butter

Beat the eggs with the yeast extract and seasoning. Add the onion and parsley. Melt the butter in a pan, pour in the mixture and stir until cooked. Serve on hot buttered toast.

BUCK RAREBIT
Cooking time 10 minutes
SERVES 2

4 eggs
175 g/6 oz cheese, grated
1 teaspoon Worcestershire
  sauce

pepper
2 slices of bread
parsley sprigs to garnish

Beat 2 eggs and mix in the cheese, Worcestershire sauce and
pepper to taste. Lightly toast the bread on both sides. Spread
the cheese mixture on to each slice of bread and grill until
the cheese melts and browns. Poach the remaining 2 eggs
(see page 149) and serve one on each toasted slice. Garnish
with parsley sprigs and serve hot.

GARLIC AND PARSLEY BREAD
Cooking time 10 minutes
Oven temperature Hot 220°C, 425°F, Gas Mark 7

100 g/4 oz butter
2 cloves garlic, crushed and
  chopped finely
1½ tablespoons fresh
  chopped parsley

black pepper
1 small French loaf or
  baguette

Beat together the butter, garlic, parsley and black pepper
until the mixture is soft. At about 1-inch intervals along the
leaf, make slanting cuts with a knife but take care not to cut
right through the bread; only about four-fifths of the way.
Spread the butter mixture into each cut, then wrap in foil
and bake in a hot oven for a few minutes. Open foil, then
return to oven for about three minutes until crisped.

This is excellent as an accompaniment to salads, pizzas or
on picnics.

SMOKY SCRAMBLE
Cooking time 3–4 minutes
SERVES 1

25 g/1 oz butter
2 eggs
1 tablespoon milk
3 tablespoons smoky bacon
flavoured TVP pieces
(such as Smokey Snaps)

salt and black pepper to taste
2 teaspoons chopped fresh
chives (optional)

Beat the eggs well in a large cup. Add the rest of the ingredients and beat a little more. Melt the butter in a saucepan and add the mixture. Stir constantly on a low heat, making sure it doesn't stick to the bottom of the pan.

When ready, serve on wholewheat toast.

GARLIC BAKED BEANS
Cooking time – under 5 minutes
SERVES 1

2 tablespoons margarine
1 clove garlic

1 220-g/7¾-oz can of baked
beans

Melt the margarine in a small saucepan. Slice the garlic thinly and fry in the margarine for a minute or two. Add the can of baked beans, stirring well to mix in the garlic. Serve on a couple of rounds of wholewheat toast.

Note: This is a very tasty and high-fibre-content meal. The frying seems to slightly neutralise the afterblast while still retaining the delicious flavour of the garlic.

CHEESY-GARLIC MUSHROOMS ON TOAST
Cooking time about 8 minutes
SERVES 1

3 tablespoons margarine
1 clove garlic, finely
  chopped
50 g/2 oz mushrooms, sliced
fresh black pepper

100 g/4 oz crumbly cheese,
  such as Lancashire
2 tablespoons milk
2 slices wholewheat bread

Fry the garlic in the margarine for a couple of minutes, then add the mushrooms and fry for a further 4–5 minutes, stirring occasionally. Season with black pepper to taste.

Meanwhile grill the cheese in a little foil tray until it is brown and bubbling.

Toast the bread, then drain the mushroom and garlic mixture and place it on the toast. Cover with the melted cheese.

Serve with a few grilled tomatoes, if wished.

SPICY SOSSY SCRUNCHIES
Cooking time 15 minutes
Makes 4

1 medium onion, chopped
  very finely
1 clove garlic, chopped
  finely
225 g/ 8 oz vegetarian
  sausagemeat (such as
  Sosmix) (reconstituted
  weight)
2 tablespoons tomato purée

3 plump tomatoes, peeled
  and chopped finely (or
  4–5 canned tomatoes,
  similarly prepared)
½ level teaspoon paprika
good pinch dry mustard
salt and pepper
1 beaten egg
golden breadcrumbs to coat

Mix together the onion, garlic, sausagemeat, tomato purée, tomatoes, paprika, mustard and seasoning. Form into four round flat shapes. Coat with the beaten egg and cover with breadcrumbs. Repeat for a good thick coating. Fry in hot oil for about 15 minutes, turning over once or twice. Dry on absorbent kitchen roll to remove excess oil.

Serve with mushrooms fried in butter or fried onions and mashed potato.

Jacket Baked Potatoes Choose large or medium potatoes, but try to make sure the potatoes you use are roughly the same size. Scrub clean, then dry and prick all over with a fork. Bake in a hot oven (220°C, 425°F, Gas Mark 7) for 1–1¼ hours until soft – depending on size. When the potatoes are cooked, make a crosswise slit on the top of each one, using a sharp knife. Squeeze the potato gently using a cloth until the cross opens at all four points. Top with a pat of butter or margarine. Serve hot, sprinkled with salt and pepper and extra butter, as required.

Serve baked potatoes with:
* Cottage cheese and chives, on their own, or with baked beans, too.
* Cream cheese and chopped onions with a side salad.
* Yogurt and chopped fresh parsley or chives.
* Shredded raw cabbage, grated raw carrot and onion blended with mayonnaise.
* Olives and gherkins.

Baked potato fillings:
When the potato is baked, scoop out some of the inside, mix with a little butter, salt and pepper and any of the following. Return the mixture to the shell and reheat in the oven before serving.

* Chopped fried tomatoes and onions.
* Sweetcorn.
* Chopped hard-boiled egg with cooked peas.
* Boiled chopped onion with crumbled cheese.
* Sautéed onions and pimento.
* Finely chopped green pepper.

TOASTY EGG SANDWICH
Cooking time 10 minutes
SERVES 2

3 eggs
salt and pepper
25 g/1 oz butter
4 large rounds of bread
2 teaspoons sandwich or
  cucumber spread

1 tablespoon finely chopped
  walnuts
cress
1 tablespoon cranberry sauce

Beat the eggs well with the salt and pepper. Heat the butter in a pan, pour in the eggs and stir until just scrambled. Cool in a bowl. Toast the bread on both sides and cover 2 slices with the sandwich spread. Pile the scrambled egg on top, adding the walnuts and cress. Cover the two remaining slices with cranberry sauce and press lightly, with the sauce side down, on to the egg filling. Serve with shredded lettuce.

SANDWICHES

Spruce up your sandwiches with these super sandwich filling suggestions – great for snacks, picnics or packed lunches . . . The sweet ones are ideal for children's parties.

Peanut Popper Spread peanut butter on lightly buttered wholewheat bread. Dribble honey over and top with sliced banana.

Beety Bite Bind together grated Lancashire cheese and cooked diced beetroot with mayonnaise. Spread on granary bread.

Granny's Sarnie Chop small crunchy pieces of a Granny Smith's apple, bind with soft cheese and sprinkle with mint.

Raspberry Relish Mix soft cheese with crushed raspberries, lemon juice and a sprinkling of brown sugar. Spread on wholewheat bread.

Peanut Granary On buttered granary bread, spread peanut butter, chopped hard-boiled egg, chopped salted celery and a dash of mustard and lemon juice.

Spring Fling Mix cream cheese with finely chopped spring onions and chopped raw carrot. Spread on buttered bread topped with crunchy radish slices.

Pimento Pick Mix cottage cheese with chopped pimento and chopped olives. Spread on buttered granary bread and top with mustard and cress.

Nutty Carrot Crunch Crush a portion of salted peanuts and add half as much again of grated raw carrot. Blend with mayonnaise and season with a little sea salt, then spread on bread.

Pineapple Punch Spread the bread with a filling of soft cheese spread blended with crushed pineapple. Sprinkle with chopped preserved ginger.

Nutty Narna Cover buttered bread with slices of banana dipped in lemon juice, then sprinkle with grated chocolate. Garnish with a piece of walnut.

Sunny Honey On buttered dark rye crispbread, spread honey and sprinkle all over with sunflower seeds. (This makes a delicious breakfast snack, too.)

French Frolic Take small slices of crusty French bread, spread with a mixture of Camembert cheese, chopped pecan nuts or similar nuts, lemon juice and Tabasco pepper sauce in softened butter.

Hot Shot Cover buttered brown bread with a filling of sliced hard-boiled egg, smothered with grated cheese and curry sauce.

Smokey Joe's Cover a slice of buttered wholewheat bread with rounds of Austrian smoked cheese. Top with thin slices of raw mushroom and corn relish.

Dutch Treat Grate some Edam cheese over a slice of bread. Top with thin slices of apple dipped in lemon juice and peeled, de-seeded crushed grapes.

Welsh Wizard Top buttered brown bread with thin slices of Caerphilly cheese, chopped raw leeks and grated eating apple in natural yogurt.

Note: To keep picnic sandwiches fresh, wrap them in lettuce leaves before packaging. This stops them drying out and prevents tainting by the flavour of the wrapping.

Try contrasting crisp and crunchy fillings with softer ones.

For sandwiches, use bread about 24 hours old – it's less likely to crumble than fresh bread.

MAKE YOUR OWN CHEESE

Try this very simple cheese recipe

HOME MADE CHEESE

600 ml/1 pint pasteurised   1 lemon
  milk   salt

You will need the following equipment lemon squeezer, saucepan, thermometer, bowl, colander, butter muslin cloths, shallow dish, perforated ladle, string, spoon.

This must be sterilised by boiling in water or use a sterilising solution (do not add metal to this solution).

Squeeze the juice from the lemon. Heat the milk to 38°C/100°F and pour into the bowl. Add the lemon juice and leave for 15 minutes for curds and whey to form.

Line the colander with dampened muslin and stand the colander in a shallow dish. Spoon the curd into the colander with the perforated ladle. Knot the corners of the cloth, hang over a bowl and leave for 30 minutes for the whey to drain. Scrape the cheese from the sides of the muslin and put in a new muslin cloth. Hang over the bowl for another 30 minutes.

Remove the cheese from the muslin. Add salt to taste and wrap in greaseproof paper.

Points to remember
Wash your hands thoroughly at first.
Keep all dairy products cool, clean and covered.
The cheese should be eaten fresh within 2–3 days and stored in a refrigerator.

Party Time

When it comes to throwing a party, whatever you do, don't pander to your non-vegetarian guests by serving meat – provide them with a good selection of tasty vegetarian fare instead.

To some extent, your culinary capabilities will be on trial; but if you can show them you don't *have* to eat meat to enjoy yourself, you might win one or two round to your way of thinking. Always aim to make the spread look as tempting and appetising as possible.

NOVELTY NOSH FOR PARTIES

Give your guests a smile with these happy-looking table novelties.

Cheery Cheesy Faces Simply spread Cornish wafers with butter and put on each a thick slice of cheese, cut round to the shape of the wafer.

Arrange stuffed olive halves for the eyes, gherkin fans for the noses and tomato wedges for upturned smiles.

CROCODILE CUCUMBER

1 cucumber	cocktail cherries
few blanched almonds	coloured cocktail onions
stuffed olives	olives
Cheddar cheese cubes	gherkins

Choose a slightly curved cucumber and cut the broad end of the cucumber lengthwise for 5–7.5 cm/2–3 inches to form the mouth, which is propped open with a small piece of cocktail stick.

Press a few pieces of blanched almonds into the 'jaws' for teeth. Arrange 2 stuffed olives for the eyes and 4 cocktail sticks for the legs. Then fix the cubes of cheese on cocktail sticks, topped with cocktail cherries, onions etc, and place down the back of the cucumber to represent spines.

CHESS BOARD

This makes two sets of chessmen: 16 pawns, 2 queens, 2 kings, 4 bishops, 4 knights and 4 castles.

100 g/4 oz Caerphilly cheese	coloured cocktail onions
100 g/4 oz Double	black olives
Gloucester cheese	stuffed olives
100 g/4 oz blue Stilton	radishes
100 g/4 oz white Stilton	

Using blue and white Stilton for one set and Caerphilly and Double Gloucester for the other, make the base of all the *chessmen* with 2 cubes of cheese. Place one cube on top of the other and secure with a cocktail stick. Spear a red, green and yellow cocktail onion on top of each one for the *pawns*. Instead of the onions, use black olives for the *knights* and stuffed olives for the *bishops*. The *castles* have a bought brightly coloured little flag on top.

Use a radish for the *King's crown* and a radish rose for the *Queen's crown*.

Arrange on a chess board on a buffet table, then stand back and watch your guests make their opening gambits.

Pyramids Butter and spread fillings on various sizes of bread circles. Stack them on top of each other – starting with the largest circle at the bottom and the smallest at the top. Vary the flavours and colours of the different fillings.

MELON MONSTER

for the dip
150 g/5 oz cream cheese
100 g/4 oz Derby cheese
3 tablespoons mayonnaise
1 tablespoon sherry
paprika

chopped chives
to decorate
1 melon
carrot
cocktail onions
celery

Cut the melon in half and scoop out the flesh. Mix this together with the cheeses, mayonnaise, sherry and a little paprika until a thick coating consistency is obtained. Add any extra suitable ingredients, such as chopped chives and celery, if liked. Pile the mixture into half the melon, sprinkle with a little extra paprika pepper and chives to garnish.

Use the other half of the melon to make a mask using a carrot (nose), cocktail onions (eyes), celery (mouth) for the face. Serve surrounded by crisps and little biscuits for spreading on.

BROWN BREAD COTTAGE

1 small brown loaf
few thin slices brown bread
225 g/8 oz Cheshire cheese
  grated

butter
1 cucumber
some tomatoes

Cut the top off the loaf, to use as a roof. Hollow out the inside of the loaf (you can use these for breadcrumbs). Butter the slices of bread, cutting off the crusts, and fill with the Cheshire cheese. Cut into miniature sandwiches and arrange inside the loaf.

'Thatch' the roof with long strips of cucumber. Use tomato halves for the edge of the roof, and cut out windows and doors using a sharp knife. Put the loaf on a base, such as a bread board or a large wooden platter, and surround with cubes of cheese on cocktail sticks.

DEVILLED CHEESE TARTS

Cooking time 25 minutes
Oven temperature Moderately Hot 200°C, 400°F, Gas Mark 6
Makes 10 tarts

for the cheese pastry
75 g/3 oz butter
175 g/6 oz plain flour
¼ teaspoon salt
pinch cayenne pepper
75 g/3 oz Lancashire cheese, grated
1 egg, beaten
1–2 tablespoons cold water
for the filling
100 g/4 oz softened butter

175 g/6 oz Lancashire cheese, grated
1 teaspoon curry powder or to taste
1 small cooking apple, peeled and grated
25 g/1 oz salted peanuts, chopped
chopped chives to garnish

To make the pastry, rub the butter into the flour, salt and cayenne pepper until the mixture resembles fine breadcrumbs. Stir in the cheese, egg and enough water to form a stiff dough. Roll out the pastry and cut out 10 shapes. Use to line small greased oval or round tins. Line each with a small piece of greaseproof paper and a few baking beans. Bake in a moderately hot oven for 15 minutes. Remove the greaseproof paper and baking beans and bake for a further 10 minutes until cooked. Remove the pastry from the tins and cool on a wire rack.

For the filling, beat all the ingredients together, except the chives, until well combined. Fill the cold pastry cases and garnish with chopped chives.

CHEESE AND POTATO BUTTONS
Cooking time 4–5 minutes
Makes about 55 buttons

75 g/3 oz softened butter
1 egg, beaten
175 g/6 oz Lancashire cheese,
  grated

275 g/10 oz mashed potato
4 tablespoons plain flour
oil for deep frying

Stir the butter, egg and cheese into the mashed potato. Add the flour and work to a stiff dough. Form into 2.5-cm/1-inch balls. Heat the oil until a 1-cm/½-inch cube of bread browns in 1 minute. Fry the buttons in the oil for 4–5 minutes until golden brown. Drain on absorbent kitchen paper. Serve hot on cocktail sticks.

THOUSAND ISLAND EGGS
SERVES 8

8 large tomatoes
600 ml/1 pint mayonnaise
3 tablespoons capers
2 tablespoons chopped fresh
  parsley
17 hard-boiled eggs

2 tablespoons tomato
  ketchup
2 teaspoons finely grated
  onion
1 cucumber
watercress

Place the tomatoes in boiling water for 1 minute, then put into cold water and remove the skins. Mix half the mayonnaise with the capers and parsley. Finely chop 1 egg, mix into the remaining mayonnaise with the tomato ketchup and onion.

Cut a thin slice from one side of each of the remaining 16 eggs, so they can stand level. Using an egg slicer, cut halfway through each egg and place in the centre of a large serving dish. Cover with the caper mayonnaise. Halve the tomatoes, arrange round the eggs and cover with the ketchup mayonnaise. Slice the unpeeled cucumber thinly and place, overlapping, around the dish. Break the cress into small bunches and use as a garnish between the eggs and tomatoes.

CREAMY CHEESE DIP

225 g/8 oz cream cheese
3 tablespoons cream or milk
½ 43-g/1½-oz packet dried
  onion soup

paprika

Beat the cream cheese and cream together until soft. Stir in the soup powder and leave to stand in a cool place for a couple of hours. Sprinkle with a little paprika and serve with small savoury biscuits, celery and carrot sticks for dipping.

CHEESE STRAWS
Cooking time 5–7 minutes
Oven temperature Moderate 180°C, 350°F, Gas Mark 4

50 g/2 oz margarine
65 g/2½ oz plain flour
pinch salt
pinch dry mustard
pinch cayenne pepper

75 g/3 oz Cheddar cheese,
  grated
egg yolk
paprika and parsley to
  garnish

Rub the margarine into the flour, salt, mustard and cayenne pepper. Add the cheese and bind into a stiff paste with the egg yolk mixed with a little cold water.

Roll out thinly and cut into straws and rings.

Place on a greased baking tray and bake in a moderate oven for 5–7 minutes. Dip one end of the straws in the paprika and place in bundles through each ring. Serve garnished with parsley.

SWEET AND SOUR CHEDDAR
Cooking time 10 minutes

1 376-g/13¼-oz can
  pineapple pieces
1 teaspoon tomato purée
1 tablespoon finely chopped
  celery
1 tablespoon cornflour

2 tablespoons vinegar
100 g/4 oz Cheddar cheese,
  diced
4 Cornish wafers, coarsely
  crushed

170

Put the pineapple pieces into a pan with the tomato purée and finely chopped celery. Mix the cornflour with the vinegar, stir into the sauce and bring to the boil. When thickened, stir in the diced Cheddar cheese and coarsely crushed wafers. Serve on wholemeal bread or a bed of shredded lettuce.

LUCKY HORSESHOE

1 long French loaf	1 bunch of celery
50 g/2 oz butter	pinch paprika
175 g/6 oz tasty cheese	

Using a sharp knife, cut the loaf, almost through, into 10 evenly spaced pieces. Spread butter on the cuts. Cut 10 wedge-shaped pieces of cheese and insert one wedge into each slit, starting at one end of the loaf and working along. Bend the loaf carefully into a horseshoe shape and sprinkle with paprika. Arrange on the party table with sticks of celery in the centre and let guests help themselves.

Cocktail Egg Filling Scramble eggs (see page 147) in the usual way, adding flavouring to taste, e.g. curry powder. Pile into tiny puff pastry vol-au-vent cases. Serve hot or cold.

MUSHROOM PATTIES
Cooking time 35 minutes
Oven temperature Hot 230°C, 450°F, Gas Mark 8
MAKES 6 PATTIES

175 g/6 oz puff pastry	25 g/1 oz plain flour
25 g/1 oz margarine	500 ml/½ pint milk
100 g/4 oz mushrooms, chopped	salt and pepper

Roll out the puff pastry to about 5 mm/¼ inch thick. Cut into 5-cm/2-inch rounds, using a plain scone cutter. Using a 2.5-cm/1-inch cutter, cut almost through each round.

Sprinkle the rounds with a little cold water and place on an ungreased baking sheet. Bake on the top shelf of a hot oven for 15–20 minutes. Carefully remove the centre ring of pastry and press in the middles slightly to make room for the mushroom mixture.

Melt the margarine, add the mushrooms and cook slowly until tender. Remove the pan from the heat, add the flour and mix well. Stir in the milk slowly, add salt and pepper and return to the heat. Stir until the mixture boils, then simmer for 2–3 minutes. Allow to cool slightly and fill the pastry cases.

Alternatively, for a quick filling use a packet of mushroom sauce mix.

Popcorn is fun for parties – especially when you pop it yourself. You can buy special popcorn kits, containing the corn and a small block of vegetable fat.

Heat the fat in a large pan, then add the corn and hold the lid firmly down. After all the 'pinging' has stopped, you will have a panful of fresh popcorn in under a minute. Just sprinkle with salt and serve.

SAUSAGE ROLLS
Cooking time about 20 minutes
Oven temperature Moderately Hot 200°C, 400°F, Gas Mark 6
MAKES 15–20 ROLLS

¼ 368-g/13-oz packet vegetarian sausage mix
pinch garlic salt

1 450 g/1 lb packet puff pastry (animal fat-free)
milk

Mix the sausage mix with 4–5 tablespoons water and a little garlic salt. Leave to stand for 5 minutes.

Roll out the pastry to 5 mm/¼ inch thick and cut into rectangles about 7.5 cm/3 inches by 10 cm/4 inches. Roll the sausagemeat into sausage shapes, place a sausage in each pastry rectangle and roll into shape, sealing the long edge well.

Prick the tops with a fork or slit with a sharp knife, and

brush the sausage rolls with a little milk. Place on a baking tray and bake in a moderately hot oven for about 20 minutes until golden brown.

TIPSY ROLLS
Cooking time about 1 hour
Oven temperature Moderately Hot 190°C, 375°F, Gas Mark 5
SERVES 4

1 onion or leek, thinly sliced	1 egg, beaten
15 g/½ oz butter	75 g/3 oz Cheddar cheese,
4 soft rolls	grated
300 ml/½ pint dry cider	pinch garlic salt
1 carrot, grated	salt and pepper to taste

Lightly fry the onion or leek in the butter. Cut a thin slice from the top of each roll and reserve. Remove the bread from inside the rolls and soak this in the cider, which has been reduced to 150 ml/¼ pint by boiling. Add the onion or leek, carrot, egg, cheese, garlic salt and seasoning and mix thoroughly. Divide the mixture between the 4 empty bread rolls and fill them. Replace the lids. Wrap the rolls in foil and bake in a moderately hot oven for about 50 minutes. Serve hot or cold.

STILTON DIP

75 g/3 oz Stilton cheese	3 tablespoons double cream
4-cm/1½-inch cucumber	salt and pepper

Crumble the Stilton into a bowl. Cut 2 slices of cucumber for garnish and finely chop the remainder. Add to the Stilton with the cream and seasoning. Garnish with the slices of cucumber and serve with savoury biscuits.

WENSLEYDALE DIP

100 g/4 oz Wensleydale
  cheese, crumbled
4 tablespoons double cream
4 walnuts, chopped

chopped watercress
pinch cayenne pepper
salt and pepper

Break up the cheese with a fork and work in the cream until a fairly soft and smooth consistency is obtained. Add the walnuts, watercress and seasonings. Serve with potato crisps.

DANISH OPEN SANDWICHES

A Danish open sandwich is more than a snack – it can be a meal in its own right.

Whatever bread you choose, cut it into square slices about 5 mm/¼ inch thick. Spread liberally with butter or margarine, then add the topping.

The following open sandwiches will form a delicious and decorative part of your party table.

The Open Wide Open Spread Tartex paste liberally on slices of bread and sprinkle with chopped chives. Arrange tomato slices in opposite corners and cucumber slices in the other two corners. Spoon chopped hard-boiled egg, seasoned with salt and pepper, in the centre. Garnish with a sprig of parsley.

Rye Smile Cover a slice of rye bread with a layer of lettuce. Top with sliced Gouda cheese and arrange alternative slices of egg and cucumber diagonally across. Place a tomato half either side and top with a radish rose.

Tommy Egg Arrange 4 slices of hard-boiled eggs, along one side of a slice of bread, slightly overlapped by 4 slices of tomato alongside. Pipe the centre with mayonnaise and sprinkle with chopped parsley.

Grape Ring Skin, halve and seed some white or black grapes. Arrange them in a circle on the slice of bread. Spoon crumbled Danish Blue cheese in the centre and top with a sprig of watercress.

Frooty Tooty Spread the bread with soft butter or

margarine and lay a lettuce leaf on. Mix natural yogurt or cream with well drained fruit salad and spoon over the lettuce leaf. Decorate with fresh orange slices or banana dipped in lemon juice.

Cheddar Capers Mix enough grated Cheddar cheese with mayonnaise and minced capers to make a paste. Spread on the bread and top with tomato slices and chopped chives.

Cheesy Pear Chomp Place a layer of lettuce on the bread. Crumble Cheshire cheese and mix with mashed cooked pear. Spoon on to the centre of the lettuce and top with chopped walnuts.

Lanky Tang Place a layer of lettuce on the bread. Mix crumbled Lancashire cheese with cream and minced or finely chopped spring onion. Spread on to the lettuce and top with a radish rose.

Mint Shake Crumble Wensleydale cheese over the slice of bread and sprinkle chopped fresh mint over it. Place a small lettuce leaf in one corner and a slice of tomato with a button mushroom either side in the other. Top the lettuce with crumbled egg yolk.

SPREAD IT AROUND

Here are some super spreads that go exceptionally well with crusty chunks of French bread, fingers of buttered whole-wheat, crispbreads, granary bread or strips of toast.

Blue Smoothy Blend 50 g/2 oz blue cheese, 50 g/2 oz soft butter, 1 tablespoon lemon juice and some black pepper to taste.

Appley Ever After Peel and grate half a medium apple and mix with 50 g/2 oz cottage cheese and 50 g/2 oz butter.

Bean Feast To a 220-g/7¾-oz can of baked beans, add 75 g/3 oz grated cheese and black pepper to taste. Mash with a fork until smooth, then spread.

Cottage Spread Add 2 tablespoons crushed pineapple and a pinch of pepper to a 142-g/5-oz carton cottage cheese. Mix well and spread.

Pepperata Blend 25 g/1 oz grated Cheshire cheese, 1 chopped lettuce leaf, ¼ red pepper, chopped, and 50 g/2 oz soft butter.

Eggspread Chop 1 hard-boiled egg and blend with 50 g/2 oz soft butter, ½ tablespoon salad cream and a little chopped fresh parsley.

Ginger–Upper Blend 1 85-g/3-oz packet of cream cheese, 2 teaspoons finely chopped stem ginger and 1 teaspoon ginger syrup.

Nutty Mayonnaise Blend 50 g/2 oz chopped walnuts, some shredded lettuce and 1 tablespoon salad dressing. Add ½ teaspoon yeast extract, if liked.

Redskinned Eggs Slice 3–4 skinned tomatoes and cook in 25 g/1 oz butter for a few minutes. Heat 2 eggs together and then stir into the tomatoes. When the mixture thickens, add salt and pepper and use when cool.

PARTY TRIFLE
Cooking time about 10 minutes
SERVES about 8

6–8 trifle sponges	50 g/2 oz castor sugar
4 tablespoons apricot or raspberry jam (or 2 tablespoons of each)	1 teaspoon cornflour
	600 ml/1 pint milk
	300 ml/½ pint double cream
150 ml/¼ pint sherry or fruit juice with liqueur	2 tablespoons milk
2 eggs	almonds and glacé cherries to decorate
2 egg yolks	

Split the sponges and fill with the jam. Cut each into three and put in the serving bowl. Pour the sherry or fruit juice over and leave to soak for 30 minutes or longer. Beat the eggs and yolks well together with the sugar and cornflour. Warm the milk and gradually mix into the egg mixture. Return to the pan (or a double boiler) and stir constantly over a low heat until creamy. Strain the warm custard over the soaked sponge and leave until cold.

Whip the cream and milk together until just thick. Spread some over the custard and pipe the rest, using a large nose nozzle, round the edge. Decorate with halved almonds and cherries.

176

GRAPEFRUIT BUBBLY
Cooking time 5 minutes
SERVES 8

2 oranges
50 g/2 oz castor sugar
2 540-g/19-fl oz cans
  grapefruit juice
6 eggs

1 241-ml/8.5-fl oz bottle
  ginger beer
2–3 ice cubes
mint leaves to decorate

Squeeze the juice from the oranges and pour into a pan, add the sugar and 4 strips of orange rind without pith. Heat gently to dissolve the sugar, then cool.

Whisk the grapefruit juice, eggs and strained orange juice together and pour into a serving jug. Add the ginger beer and ice cubes just before serving. Top with mint leaves.

HOT COFFEE CREAM WITH BRANDY
Cooking time 5 minutes
SERVES 8

6 eggs
100 g/4 oz castor sugar
4 tablespoons brandy
600 ml/1 pint milk
600 ml/1 pint strong black
  coffee

4 tablespoons double cream,
  lightly whipped
25 g/1 oz plain chocolate,
  grated

Whisk the eggs and sugar together with the brandy. Heat the milk and coffee to just boiling point, then gradually whisk it into the eggs. Serve hot, topping each drink with lightly whipped cream and grated chocolate.

Puddings and Desserts

MERINGUE AND STRAWBERRY SNOW
Cooking time 45 minutes–1 hour
Oven temperature Moderate 180°C, 350°F, Gas Mark 4

SERVES 8

4 egg whites
225 g/8 oz castor sugar
little butter

150 ml/¼ pint double cream
225 g/8 oz strawberries,
    fresh or frozen

Whisk the egg whites stiffly, then sprinkle in 2 tablespoons castor sugar and whisk again. Add half of the sugar in this way, then fold in the remainder.

Butter the inside of a 1–1.25-litre/1½–2-pint ovenproof basin and coat with castor sugar. Fill with the meringue and stand the basin in a baking tin filled to a depth of 4 cm/1½ inches with hot water. Bake on the shelf below centre in a moderate oven for 45 minutes–1 hour. When cooked, the meringue will be coloured on top, well risen and firm to the touch. Remove from the baking tin and leave for 10 minutes, then turn the basin upside down over a serving dish and lift off when cool.

Whip the cream until thick and halve or slice the strawberries. Cover the meringue with the cream and decorate with the strawberries.

BUTTERSCOTCH SEMOLINA PUDDING
Cooking time 8–10 minutes

SERVES 4

generous 600 ml/1 pint milk
25 g/1 oz butter
2 tablespoons brown sugar
4 teaspoons golden syrup

4 tablespoons semolina
25 g/1 oz peanut brittle,
    crushed

Heat together the milk, butter, sugar and syrup. Sprinkle the

178

semolina on the milk and simmer for 3–4 minutes, stirring all the time. When the mixture thickens, remove from the heat. Serve hot or cold in individual dishes, sprinkled with the peanut brittle.

BANANA OMELETTE FLAMBÉ
Cooking time about 10 minutes
SERVES 2

15 g/½ oz butter
2 bananas, thinly sliced
grated rind and juice of ½
  lemon

1 tablespoon brown sugar
2 omelettes (see page 141)
icing sugar
2 tablespoons brandy

Melt the butter and add the sliced bananas, lemon rind and juice, brown sugar and cook gently until just soft. Place half the banana filling along the fold line of each cooked omelette. Turn out on to a heated serving dish, sprinkle the top with icing sugar and glaze under a very hot grill. For each omelette, pour 1 tablespoon warm brandy over the top, ignite and serve at once.

WELSH APPLE FLAN
Cooking time 35 minutes
Oven temperature Moderately Hot 200°C, 400°F, Gas Mark 6
SERVES 4–5

150 g/5 oz shortcrust pastry
450 g/1 lb cooking apples,
  peeled, cored and diced
50 g/2 oz demerara sugar
½ teaspoon ground
  cinnamon

5 tablespoons water
1 lemon yogurt
50 g/2 oz Caerphilly cheese,
  grated
1 glacé cherry

Roll out the pastry and use to line an 18-cm/7-inch flan ring. Bake blind (see page 89) in a moderately hot oven for 20 minutes. Cook the apples in a pan with the sugar, cinnamon and water until soft, then sieve or liquidise. Add the yogurt and grated cheese to the apple purée and pile into the flan case. Sprinkle with demerara sugar and top with the glacé cherry. Serve cold with fresh whipped cream.

FROZEN ORANGE MOUSSE
Cooking time 10–15 minutes
SERVES 4

scant 150 ml/¼ pint orange
  juice
pinch salt
100 g/4 oz castor sugar

3 egg yolks
150 ml/¼ pint double
  cream, lightly whipped

Heat the orange juice, salt and sugar in the top of a double saucepan or in a bowl over a pan of simmering water. Beat the egg yolks until thick and lemon-coloured and add to the orange mixture. Cook until thick, stirring constantly. Cool and fold in the cream. Pour into individual glasses, then place in the freezing compartment of a refrigerator before serving.

HONEYED BAKED BANANAS
Cooking time 20–30 minutes
Oven temperature Moderate 160°C, 325°F, Gas Mark 3
SERVES 1

2 bananas
little lemon juice

1 teaspoon brown sugar
1 tablespoon honey

Place the whole bananas in an ovenproof dish and sprinkle with lemon juice and brown sugar. Trickle honey lengthways over each banana, then bake in a moderate oven for 20–30 minutes.

TREACLE AND PEAR TART
Cooking time 35 minutes
Oven temperature Moderately Hot 200°C, 400°F, Gas Mark 6, then
Moderate 180°C, 350°F, Gas Mark 6

SERVES 4

3–4 dessert pears
225 g/8 oz shortcrust pastry
50 g/2 oz margarine
50 g/2 oz demerara sugar

1½ teaspoons golden syrup
100 g/4 oz quick-cooking
  porridge oats

Peel, core and quarter the pears. Line a 20-cm/8-inch flan ring with the shortcrust pastry and arrange the pears in the pastry case. Melt the margarine and add the demerara sugar, golden syrup and porridge oats. Blend the mixture and pour over the pears, making sure the pears are covered with the mixture. Bake in a moderately hot oven for 15 minutes then reduce the temperature to moderate for a further 15 minutes. Serve with cream.

COFFEE POTS
Cooking time about 30 minutes
Oven temperature Moderate 160°C, 325°F, Gas Mark 3

SERVES 4

450 ml/¾ pint milk
1 tablespoon instant coffee
  powder

2 tablespoons castor sugar
3 eggs, beaten
chopped walnuts to decorate

Heat the milk, pour on the coffee and sugar, and stir until dissolved. Whisk in the beaten eggs. Strain into 4 ramekin dishes and place in a baking tin. Fill the tin with warm water to come halfway up the sides of the dishes. Bake in a moderate oven for 20 minutes or until firm. Serve hot or cold, decorated with chopped walnuts.

GRAPE WHISPER

225 g/8 oz green and black grapes
2 tablespoons white wine

3 egg whites
75 g/3 oz castor sugar

Cut the grapes in half and remove the pips. Soak the grape halves in the wine, turning them from time to time. Whisk the egg whites stiffly and gradually whisk in the sugar. Fold in the grapes and spoon into individual glasses. Serve within 30 minutes with wafer biscuits.
Note: Make up this dessert just before it is needed.

YOGURT MALLOW

2 egg whites
50 g/2 oz castor sugar
1 150-g/5.3-oz carton natural yogurt

1 tablespoon toasted coconut

Whisk the egg whites stiffly, then gradually whisk in the sugar. Fold in the yogurt carefully and spoon the mixture into glasses. Sprinkle with coconut and serve within 30 minutes. Add pieces of chopped fresh fruit, if wished.
Note: Make up dessert just before serving.

PATAGONIA CREAM TART
Cooking time 35–40 minutes
Oven temperature 180°C, 350°F, Gas Mark 4
SERVES 4

100 g/4 oz shortcrust pastry
3 egg whites
300 ml/½ pint double cream

pinch nutmeg
few drops vanilla essence
1 tablespoon brown sugar

Line a pie plate with the shortcrust pastry. Mix the whipped egg whites with the cream, nutmeg, vanilla essence and sugar. Pour the mixture into the dish and bake in a moderate oven for 35–40 minutes.

A layer of sultanas can be placed at the base of the tart before adding the cream mixture, or a cover of pastry may be placed on top of the cream.

JAMAICAN DELIGHT
Cooking time 10 minutes
SERVES 4

50 g/2 oz milk chocolate
3 teaspoons molasses
2 eggs, separated

2–3 teaspoons rum
4 bananas
flaked almonds to decorate

Melt the chocolate in a basin over hot water. When melted, stir in the molasses. Remove from the heat and stir in the egg yolks and rum. Whisk the whites until stiff and fold into the mixture.

Cut each banana in half lengthwise and cut each portion into 2 pieces. Place in 4 individual serving dishes, pour the chocolate sauce over and decorate with flaked almonds.

HONEY-GLAZED BAKED PEARS
Cooking time about 25 minutes
Oven temperature Moderate 180°C, 350°F, Gas Mark 4
SERVES 4

4 dessert pears
4 tablespoons honey
4 cloves
25 g/1 oz butter

for the syrup
1 tablespoon honey
6 tablespoons hot water

Peel, halve and core the pears. Place in baking dish and fill the centres with honey, a clove and top with a knob of butter.

For the syrup, dissolve the honey in the hot water. Spoon the syrup into the baking dish and bake in a moderate oven for about 25 minutes, basting occasionally.

DAMSON VALLEY CRUMBLE
Cooking time 20–25 minutes
Oven temperature Moderately Hot 190°C, 375°F, Gas Mark 5
SERVES 4

* The Damson Valley referred to in the name of the recipe refers to the Lyth Valley in the Lake District where, at the end of the summer, roadside stallkeepers sell damsons picked fresh from the orchards that fill the valley. They are reputed to have been first grown by the monks at Cartmel Abbey many hundreds of years ago by grafting wild sloes with wild plums. Whatever their history may be, they are the tastiest damsons you will ever encounter . . . superb in jams, crumbles, wine – or eaten fresh.

450 g/1 lb damsons
40 g/1½ oz brown sugar
3 tablespoons water
3 tablespoons brandy
    (optional)
For the crumble
175 g/6 oz medium oatmeal

75 g/3 oz butter
4 tablespoons brown sugar
½ teaspoon sea salt
6 tablespoons chopped
    sunflower seeds
grated nutmeg

Wash the fruit, then cut in half and remove stones. Place in an ovenproof dish and sprinkle with the brown sugar, water and brandy.

Make the crumble by mixing the oatmeal, butter, sugar, salt and sunflower seeds together until a crumb-like consistency is achieved. Spread the topping over the fruit, pat down slightly and sprinkle with a little grated nutmeg. Bake in a moderately hot oven for 20–25 minutes until the top is turning golden brown. Serve with ice-cream or single cream.

MUESLI
SERVES 1

2 tablespoons rolled oats
1 eating apple
juice of ½ lemon
2 tablespoons sweetened
   condensed milk or honey
1 teaspoon chopped almonds
1 teaspoon raisins

1 teaspoon grated nuts
1 tablespoon fresh fruit
   segments, according to
   season, or presoaked dried
   fruit
1 tablespoon wheat germ or
   bran

Put the oats in a bowl, adding enough water to cover and leave overnight. Before serving, grate the apple into the oats and add the lemon juice. Stir in the condensed milk or honey, then add the remaining ingredients.

Baking

WHOLEWHEAT BREAD – QUICK AND SIMPLE
Baking time about 45 minutes
Oven temperatures Hot 230°C, 450°F, Gas Mark 8 then
Moderate 180°C, 350°F, Gas Mark 4

25 g/1 oz yeast
1 tablespoon honey (or
 brown sugar)
½ crushed vitamin C tablet
 (optional)
300 ml/½ pint warm water

450 g/1 lb wholewheat flour
 (stoneground and
 organically-grown for
 preference).
¼ teaspoon sea salt
25 g/1 oz margarine

Cream the yeast and honey together in a basin (use a fork) and add the vitamin C and 150 ml/¼ pint warm water. Cover and leave in a warm place until the yeast begins to foam and 'sing'.

Meanwhile mix together the wholewheat flour, salt and margarine. Then pour on the yeast and work into the flour. Add the rest of the water a little at a time until the dough is pliable. Knead on a floured surface for 5 minutes or more, giving it a really good going over. Place in a 2 lb bread tin which has been greased with margarine. Cover with a clean tea towel and allow to rise in a warm place for 20–25 minutes until about doubled in size. Brush top with a little milk to glaze. Put in a hot oven. After 10 minutes, turn the heat down to moderate.

Test to see if the loaf is ready by taking it out of the tin and tapping it on the bottom. If it sounds hollow, it is ready. Turn off the oven but return the loaf to the oven (out of the tin) for 5 minutes to crisp up, after glazing with a little milk.

Points to note You can replace 50 g/2 oz of the wholewheat flour with soya flour to add extra protein.

You can use instant dried yeast, which you just stir into the flour instead of creaming separately first.

You can make onion bread by simply taking a chunk of

dough and working into it thinly sliced onion rings before allowing to rise. This is absolutely scrumptious.

But above all *please* make your own bread at least once a week. It fills the house with a mouthwatering aroma, it's full of goodness, it's delicious . . . and it's *yours*.

GRANNY JONES'S PARKIN

(Parkin is a northern traditional sweet treat served on Bonfire night)

Cooking time 50 minutes
Oven temperature Moderate 180°C, 350°F, Gas Mark 4

175 g/6 oz wholewheat flour
175 g/6 oz oatmeal
1 teaspoon ground ginger
100 g/4 oz brown sugar
1 egg

little milk
100 g/4 oz margarine
2 tablespoons black treacle
1½ tablespoons golden
  syrup

Mix the flour, oatmeal, ginger and sugar in a large mixing bowl. Beat in the egg and add a little milk. Melt the margarine and stir in the black treacle and syrup. Mix well into the other ingredients in the mixing bowl. Place the mixture in a greased 30 × 20-cm/12 × 8-inch baking tray. Bake in a moderate oven for 50 minutes. Serve sliced and buttered.

RICH DROP SCONES
Cooking time about 6 minutes
SERVES 4–6

50 g/2 oz butter
100 g/4 oz wholewheat flour
pinch salt
25 g/1 oz brown sugar

2 eggs, beaten
150 ml/¼ pint buttermilk or
  milk

Rub the butter into the flour and salt. Stir in the sugar, then gradually add the eggs and milk, beating well to make a smooth batter. Bake either on a griddle, heavy based frying pan or hot plate. (The cooking surface should feel hot when your hand is held just above it.) Grease the surface lightly with oil or cooking fat and drop tablespoons of the mixture on. Cook until bubbles appear on the surface and the underside is lightly browned. Turn and cook the other side. Serve warm spread with butter.

GINGERBREAD
Cooking time 50 minutes
Oven temperature Moderate 160°C, 325°F, Gas Mark 3

4 tablespoons golden syrup	pinch salt
4 tablespoons black treacle	2 teaspoons ground ginger
75 g/3 oz butter	1 teaspoon mixed spice
50 g/2 oz demerara sugar	2 eggs
100 g/4 oz wholewheat flour	1 teaspoon marmalade
100 g/4 oz self-raising flour	

Put the syrup, treacle, butter and sugar into a saucepan and heat gently without boiling, stirring until the ingredients are melted. Leave to cool. Mix the flours, salt and spices in a bowl. Beat the eggs lightly and stir thoroughly into the flour with marmalade and melted treacle mixture.

Spread into a greased 23 × 18-cm/9 × 7-inch tin. Bake in the centre of a moderate oven for 45–50 minutes. Do not disturb while cooking. When cooked, the surface should be springy to the touch. Cool for a while in the tin and turn out on to a wire rack.
Note: Some chopped crystallised ginger, 50 g/2 oz sultanas or chopped almonds may be added as extra ingredients.

WALNUT TEA LOAF
Cooking time about 40 minutes
Oven temperature Moderate 180°C, 350°F, Gas Mark 4

225 g/8 oz self-raising flour	50 g/2 oz walnuts, finely
pinch salt	chopped
50 g/2 oz butter	2 eggs
75 g/3 oz soft brown sugar	about 5 tablespoons milk

Sift the flour and salt into a bowl, rub in the butter and mix in sugar and chopped walnuts. Whisk the eggs lightly and stir into the mixture with enough milk to make a soft dough.

Spread the mixture into a greased 0.5-kg/1-lb loaf tin and bake in the centre of a moderate oven until golden brown and well risen. Cool on a wire rack.

This cake is best eaten fresh but after a few days' keeping, you can cut thick slices, toast it and spread with butter or margarine.

BULGARIAN ORANGE CAKE

100 g/4 oz butter
175 g/6 oz castor sugar
2 eggs, beaten
½-178-ml/6¼ -oz drum
  frozen concentrated
  orange juice
1 150-g/5.3-oz carton natural
  yogurt

175 g/6 oz self-raising flour
for the orange topping
50 g/2 oz butter
175 g/6 oz icing sugar, sifted
½ drum of frozen
  concentrated orange juice
some crystallised orange
  slices to decorate

Cream together the butter and sugar until light and fluffy. Beat the eggs in, then mix in the thawed orange juice and yogurt. Fold in the flour and mix lightly but thoroughly. Put the mixture into two greased and lined 18-cm/7-inch sandwich tins and smooth level. Bake in a moderately hot oven for 30 minutes or until firm and golden. Allow to cool.

To make the topping, soften the butter and beat in the icing sugar. Stir in just enough thawed orange juice to give a soft consistency. Sandwich the cakes together with a little orange topping and use the remainder to spread on the top. Decorate with the crystallised orange slices.

HONEY CHEESECAKE

Cooking time 1 hour
Oven temperature Moderate 180°C, 350°F, Gas Mark 4

175 g/6 oz digestive biscuits,
    crushed
50 g/2 oz walnuts, chopped
75 g/3 oz butter, melted
675 g/1½ lb cottage cheese
3 eggs

175 g/6 oz honey
50 g/2 oz castor sugar
2 tablespoons flour
whipped cream and
    strawberries to decorate

Combine the biscuit crumbs, chopped walnuts and melted butter. Press firmly over the base of an 18-cm/7-inch loose-bottomed cake tin lined with foil. Chill while preparing the cheesecake mixture.

Press the cottage cheese through a sieve into a bowl and beat in the eggs, one at a time. Add the honey and sugar and beat until smooth. Fold in the flour and turn the mixture into the crumb base. Bake in a moderate oven for 1 hour. Leave the cake in the oven with the heat turned off and the oven door opened until the cake is cold.

Decorate with whipped cream and strawberries before serving.

PINEAPPLE CRUNCHY CAKE

Cooking time 5 minutes
SERVES 4–6

175 g/6 oz digestive biscuits,
    crushed
75 g/3 oz butter
25 g/1 oz castor sugar
for the filling
300 ml/½ pint double cream
1 150-g/5.3-oz carton
    pineapple yogurt

25 g/1 oz almonds, chopped
1 226-g/8-oz can pineapple
    cubes
1 chocolate flake and glacé
    cherries to decorate

Melt the butter, add the sugar and biscuit crumbs and mix well. Press into a buttered 18-cm/7-inch pie plate and leave to chill.

Whip the cream until thick and mix half with the yoghurt and add the chopped almonds. Spread some of the remaining cream over the biscuit base. Arrange the pineapple cubes on the top and cover with the yogurt filling. Decorate with the remaining cream, chocolate flake and glacé cherries. Chill before serving.

MRS D'S CHOCOLATE WHOLEWHEAT CAKE
Cooking time 25–30 minutes
Oven temperature Moderate 180°C, 350°F, Gas Mark 4

100 g/4 oz butter or margarine
100 g/4 oz brown sugar
2 eggs, beaten
150 g/5 oz wholewheat flour
2 tablespoons unsweetened cocoa powder
1 teaspoon baking powder
for the filling
175 g/6 oz brown sugar
100 g/4 oz margarine

50 g/2 oz unsweetened cocoa powder
1 large banana
juice of ½ orange or lemon
for the topping
225 g/8 oz plain chocolate, melted
150–300 ml/¼–½ pint whipped cream
1 chocolate flake

Cream the butter or margarine and sugar until smooth. Beat in the eggs, one at a time to prevent curdling. Fold in the flour, to which the cocoa powder and baking powder have been added. Pour into a greased sandwich tin, base-lined with greased paper. Bake in a moderate oven for 25–30 minutes.

For the filling, mix the sugar, margarine and cocoa powder together to form a smooth paste. Cut the cake in half and spread the filling on the bottom half. Place banana slices on top and sprinkle with the orange or lemon juice.

Sandwich the cake together and spread the melted chocolate evenly on top. Spoon on the cream and make swirls using the back of a spoon. Finally, sprinkle with crumbled chocolate flake.

DATE AND COFFEE CAKES
Cooking time 20 minutes
Oven temperature Moderately Hot 190°C, 375°F, Gas Mark 5
Makes 12–14 cakes

100 g/4 oz castor sugar
2 eggs, beaten
100 g/4 oz butter
1 tablespoon coffee powder, dissolved in 1 tablespoon boiling water or 2 tablespoons coffee essence

100 g/4 oz self-raising flour
50 g/2 oz dates, chopped
pinch salt
1 teaspoon icing sugar

Beat together the sugar, eggs, butter, coffee mixture, flour, dates and salt in a bowl for a few minutes until quite smooth. Divide the mixture between 12–14 paper cases or greased patty tins and bake in a moderately hot oven for 20 minutes. Cool on a wire tray and dredge with sifted icing sugar.

LYNN'S CHERRY COCONUT CAKE
Cooking time 30 minutes
Oven temperature Moderate 180°C, 350°F, Gas Mark 4

100 g/4 oz plain cooking chocolate
50 g/2 oz margarine
100 g/4 oz desiccated coconut

100 g/4 oz castor sugar
50 g/2 oz glacé cherries, chopped
1 egg, beaten

Line an 18-cm/7-inch baking tin with foil. Gently melt the chocolate, pour into the tin and leave to set. Melt the margarine and add coconut, sugar and cherries. Mix the ingredients thoroughly with the beaten egg and spread evenly over the chocolate. Bake in a moderate oven for 30 minutes. Leave to cool before cutting into squares.

FLORRIE'S COCONUT LOAF
Cooking time 50 minutes
Oven temperature Moderate 180°C, 350°F, Gas Mark 4

100 g/4 oz margarine
100 g/4 oz castor sugar
1 egg, beaten

100 g/4 oz plain flour
50 g/2 oz desiccated coconut
little milk

Cream the margarine and sugar until smooth. Beat in the egg and add the flour, coconut and a little milk. Mix well and put in a well greased 0.5-kg/1-lb loaf tin. Bake in a moderate oven for 50 minutes.

HONEY NUT BAKE
Cooking time 50–60 minutes
Oven temperature Moderate 180°C, 350°F, Gas Mark 4
Makes 10–12 slices

25 g/1 oz butter
1 teaspoon grated lemon
  rind
175 g/6 oz honey
1 egg
100 g/4 oz plain flour

1 teaspoon baking powder
1 tablespoon milk
50 g/2 oz walnuts, chopped
50 g/2 oz dried apricots,
  chopped

Cream together the butter, lemon rind and honey. Add the egg and beat well. Sift the plain flour and baking powder twice. Fold into the mixture alternately with the milk, walnuts and apricots. Turn the mixture into a greased 0.5-kg/1-lb loaf tin and bake in a moderate oven for 50–60 minutes. Serve warm or cold with butter.

BUTTER BUBBLES
Cooking time about 8 minutes
Makes 48 squares

100 g/4 oz butter
4 tablespoons honey
175 g/6 oz castor sugar
100 g/4 oz cooking
  chocolate, grated

40 g/1½ oz desiccated
  coconut
150 g/5 oz crispy rice cereal

Grease two oblong trays with butter. Place the butter, honey and sugar in a pan. Dissolve slowly and boil for 3 minutes without stirring. Place the chocolate, coconut and rice cereal in a bowl. Pour the honey butter mixture over the cereal and stir until well mixed. Press this mixture into the two trays and cut into squares when firm.

SULTANA OAT SHORTIES
Cooking time 12–15 minutes
Oven temperature Moderate 180°C, 350°F, Gas Mark 4
Makes 24 shorties

75 g/3 oz butter
4 tablespoons honey
1 egg, beaten
50 g/2 oz self-raising flour
pinch salt

115 g/4½ oz uncooked
    rolled oats
150 g/5 oz sultanas
50 g/2 oz walnuts, chopped

Cream the butter and honey together, then beat in the egg. Sift the flour and salt together and add to the creamed mixture, with the oats, sultanas and nuts. Mix well. Form into small balls, place on a greased baking tray and flatten with a fork. Bake in a moderate oven for 12–15 minutes.

HONEY MEAL SCONES
Cooking time 10–12 minutes
Oven temperature Hot 230°C, 450°F, Gas Mark 8
Makes 12 scones

1 egg, beaten
2 tablespoons honey
100 g/4 oz wholemeal self-
    raising flour
100 g/4 oz white self-raising
    flour

½ teaspoon cinnamon
¼ teaspoon nutmeg
½ teaspoon salt
15 g/½ oz butter
about 6 tablespoons milk

Beat the egg and honey together. Mix together the flours, spices and salt. Rub the butter in lightly. Add the egg and honey mixture, then the milk. Mix to a soft dough, adding a little extra milk, if necessary. Knead lightly on a floured board until smooth. Roll or pat out to 2 cm/¾ inch thickness. Cut into 12 rounds and arrange close together on a greased baking tray. Bake in a hot oven for 10–12 minutes. Serve warm with butter.

TEA BREAD
Cooking time 1–1¼ hours
Oven temperature Moderate 180°C, 350°F, Gas Mark 4

225 g/8 oz mixed sultanas, currants, raisins and peel	1–1½ tablespoons molasses
150 ml/¼ pint cold tea	1 tablespoon water
50 g/2 oz brown sugar	1 size 1 or 2 egg, beaten
	225 g/8 oz self-raising flour

Place the dried fruit, tea and sugar in a basin and leave to soak overnight. Stir in the molasses and water. Add the beaten egg, mix well together and stir in the flour. Turn into a greased loaf tin and bake in a moderate oven for 1–1¼ hours until well risen.

NUTTY LOAF
Cooking time about 1¼ hours
Oven temperature Cool 150°C, 300°F, Gas Mark 2
Makes 12–16 slices

100 g/4 oz dried apricots, chopped	4 tablespoons honey
100 g/4 oz mixed nuts, chopped	2 eggs
150 g/5 oz sultanas	6 tablespoons milk
100 g/4 oz castor sugar	*for the topping*
350 g/12 oz self-raising flour	50 g/2 oz whole mixed nuts
	50 g/2 oz sugar
	2 tablespoons water

Put the apricots in a bowl and cover with boiling water. Leave for 10 minutes, then drain. Mix the apricots, nuts, sultanas, sugar and flour together in a bowl. Place the honey in a basin with the eggs and milk and beat together. Add to the flour mixture and mix well. Add a little more milk if the mixture is too stiff. Spoon the mixture into a greased and lined loaf tin. Bake in a cool oven for about 1¼ hours. When cooked, the loaf should have begun to shrink from the sides of the tin. Turn out and cool.

For the topping, toast the nuts lightly. Put the sugar and water in a pan over a moderate heat and stir until dissolved. Bring to the boil and boil for 1 minute. Remove from the heat, add the nuts and stir. Cool a little and spread over the top of the loaf. Serve the loaf sliced and buttered.

OATCAKES
Baking time 15 minutes
Oven temperature Moderate 180°C, 350°F, Gas Mark 4
Makes about 12

225 g/8 oz medium oatmeal
¼ teaspoon bicarbonate of soda

1 level teaspoon of salt
50 g/2 oz butter
some boiling water

Mix together the oatmeal, bicarbonate of soda and salt. Then add the butter and a little boiling water. Knead to a softish dough. Cover your rolling surface with oatmeal and roll out the dough thinly (just under ¼ inch thick). Cut into triangles and bake in a moderate oven for 15 minutes or so. They are ready when slightly brown. Cool and store in a dry place.

Serve with a little butter or margarine on top, spread with your favourite cheese or perhaps a little home-made jam.

Fresh Fruit Guide

Increasing your consumption of fresh fruit is another important step in becoming a vegetarian or vegan. As well as providing good natural roughage, fruit is an excellent source of vitamins and minerals.

Fruit is very low in fats and carbohydrates and should be substituted as often as possible for cakes, confectionery and other sweet foods.

STORING FRUIT

Apples (all dessert varieties and cookers) Store in the bottom of the refrigerator to keep crisp. Remove an hour before required.

Apricots and plums Unripe fruit will normally ripen to full flavour when kept for a day or two at room temperature.

Avocados When ripe, they will yield to gentle pressure in the hand. To ripen, wrap in newspaper and keep at room temperature for two to three days. Store in the bottom of the refrigerator for three to four days. If cut, brush the flesh with lemon juice, leave in the stone and wrap in airtight foil.

Bananas Ripen green-tipped and yellow bananas in a warm room. When brown spots appear, the pulp has become softer and more mellow, and the banana is ready to eat. NEVER put bananas in the refrigerator as this will destroy the flavour.

Blackcurrants, Blackberries and Redcurrants Best used within 24 hours of purchase or picking. Remove any cellophane covering and take out any damaged or bruised fruit. Do not wash or hull until required. Keep in the refrigerator until an hour before using.

Citrus (Oranges, grapefruit, lemons, tangerines and satsumas) Choose firm, heavy fruit with a bright, shiny skin. They will keep for one to two weeks in a cool place.

Dates Fresh dates can be kept in the refrigerator for several days. Before serving, allow to come to room temperature.

Figs These are a very fragile fruit and should be stored at room temperature for no more than 24 hours.

Gooseberries Remove bruised ones immediately. Cooking gooseberries can be kept in the refrigerator for three days but dessert gooseberries are best eaten on the day of purchase.

Grapes They should be eaten when firm and fresh. Handle carefully. Grapes are best kept in the salad drawer of a refrigerator until required.

Kiwifruit (Chinese Gooseberries) This unusual fruit has a furry brown skin and bright green flesh inside with tiny black seeds. The fruit is ripe when it is soft to the touch. To ripen, put in a bag with an apple and keep at room temperature for a few days.

Lychees These have a hard shell which protects them naturally. They can be stored at room temperature and are best eaten within four days of purchasing.

Mangoes and Paw Paws The skin should be firm and unblemished and yield to gentle pressure. Eat within two to three days of purchasing.

Melons (Honeydew, Ogen etc.) To test if a melon is ripe, press your thumb gently into the end opposite the calyx. If ripe, use within three days.

Peaches, Persimmons, Sharon Fruit and Nectarines Eat ripe fruit on the day of purchase. Under-ripe ones will ripen at room temperature.

Pears These are usually sold hard and, apart from Williams variety, can be kept in that condition in the refrigerator for a week or two. To ripen, put the pears in a warm room until there is a slight softening near the stalk. Eat within a few days when ripe.

Pineapples These are ripe when a leaf can easily be pulled out. A pineapple should be eaten within 24 hours of buying. An under-ripe one will ripen within two to three days at room temperature.

Raspberries and Strawberries These are best used within a day of purchasing. Remove any damaged fruit immediately and do not wash or hull until required. Keep in the refrigerator until an hour before using.

Rhubarb Choose sticks which are firm and snap cleanly.

Keep in a cool place such as the bottom of the refrigerator and use within three days of purchasing.

Watermelon If buying whole, make sure it is firm. Cut slices should be wrapped in foil. This way, they remain fresh for up to a week in the refrigerator.

Points to Remember Never overcook fruit. Always wash thoroughly, if necessary. Eat plenty!

WHAT'S IN SEASON?

* Denotes the beginning of the main season.

January *Home grown:* apples, cooking apples, pears, rhubarb*. *Imported:* apples, apricots, avocados, bananas, dates, grapefruit, grapes, lemons, lychees, mangoes, melons, oranges, passion fruit, peaches*, pears, pineapples, plums*, satsumas, Seville oranges, sharon fruit, strawberries, temples.

February *Home grown:* apples, cooking apples, pears, rhubarb. *Imported:* apples, avocados, bananas, clementines, dates, grapefruit, grapes, lemons, limes*, lychees, mangoes, melons, nectarines*, oranges, peaches, pears, pineapples, plums, satsumas, Seville oranges, sharon fruit, strawberries, temples.

March *Home grown:* apples, cooking apples, pears, rhubarb. *Imported*: apples, avocados, bananas, dates, grapefruit, grapes, lemons, limes, lychees, mangoes, melons, oranges, passion fruit, peaches, pears, pineapples, plums, satsumas, strawberries.

April *Home grown:* cooking apples, rhubarb, strawberries*. *Imported:* apples, apricots, avocados, bananas, cherries*, dates, grapefruit, grapes, lemons, limes, lychees, mandarins, mangoes, melons, oranges, passion fruit, peaches, pears, pineapples, plums, strawberries.

May *Home grown:* cooking apples, gooseberries*, rhubarb, strawberries.
Imported: apples, apricots*, avocados, bananas, dates, grapefruit, grapes, kiwifruit*, lemons, limes, lychees, mangoes, melons, oranges, paw paws*, peaches, pears, pineapples, plums, strawberries, watermelons*.

199

June *Home grown:* cherries★, gooseberries, raspberries★, strawberries.
Imported: apricots, apples, avocados, bananas, cherries★, dates, fresh figs★, grapefruit, grapes, gooseberries, kiwifruit, lemons, limes, lychees, mangoes, melons, nectarines★, oranges, paw paws, peaches, pears, pineapples, plums, strawberries, watermelons.

July *Home grown:* blackberries★, blackcurrants★, cherries, gooseberries, loganberries★, raspberries, redcurrants★, strawberries.
Imported: apples, apricots, avocados, bananas, cherries, dates, fresh figs, grapefruit, grapes, kiwifruit, lemons, limes, mangoes, melons, nectarines, oranges, paw paws, peaches, pears, pineapples, plums, watermelons.

August *Home grown:* apples★, blackberries, plums★, raspberries, strawberries.
Imported: apples, apricots, avocados, bananas, dates, fresh figs, grapefruit, grapes, greengages★, kiwifruit, lemons, mangoes, melons, nectarines, oranges, peaches, pears, plums, pineapples, strawberries, watermelons.

September *Home grown:* apples, cooking apples★, blackberries, pears★, plums, strawberries.
Imported: apples, avocados, bananas, dates, fresh figs, grapefruit, grapes, greengages, kiwifruit, lemons, mangoes, melons, oranges, passion fruit, paw paws, peaches, pears, pineapples, plums, pomegranates★, watermelons.

October *Home grown:* apples, cooking apples, pears, strawberries.
Imported: apples, avocados, bananas, dates, fresh figs, grapefruit, grapes, kiwifruit, lemons, mangoes, melons, oranges, passion fruit, paw paws, pears, pineapples, plums, pomegranates.

November *Home grown:* apples, cooking apples, pears.
Imported: apples, avocados, bananas, clementines, dates, grapefruit, grapes, kiwifruit, lemons, mangoes, melons, oranges, passion fruit, paw paws, persimmons★, pineapples, pomegranates, satsumas★.

December *Home grown:* apples, cooking apples, pears.
Imported: apples, apricots, avocados, bananas, clementines, cranberries, dates, grapefruit, grapes, lemons, lychees★,

mangoes, melons, oranges, passion fruit, paw paws, peaches, pears, persimmons, pineapples, pomegranates, satsumas, sharon fruit*.

FRUIT AND VITAMINS

Vitamin A Apricots and peaches are good sources. Also present in avocados, blackcurrants, gooseberries and melon.
Vitamin B Group Small quantities in apples, bananas, avocados and fresh dates.
Vitamin C Blackcurrants and kiwifruit are high in vitamin C, but more usual sources are oranges and strawberries or other fruits like avocados, melons, lemons, gooseberries, grapefruit and raspberries.
Iron Found in blackcurrants, avocados, fresh dates, apples and apricots.
Calcium Fresh dates and blackcurrants contain a great deal of calcium.

Fresh Vegetable Guide

Fresh vegetables in your daily diet play an essential role in adding nutritive goodness in a tasty and economical way. They should be eaten raw as often as possible, as cooking will inevitably destroy some of the vitamin content.

BUYING AND STORING

Aubergines Buy firm, smooth glossy aubergines and avoid soft or shrivelled ones. Store in a cool place or the bottom of a refrigerator for up to a week.

Beans These should be unblemished and should snap easily. Store in a cool place and use within three days.

Brussels Sprouts The ones to avoid are the yellowish sprouts. The best are firm and tightly-packed 'buttons'. Remove any wilted and discoloured leaves before storing. Store in a cool place and use within three or four days.

Cabbage Choose heads that are firm, plump and crisp. Store in a cool place for up to four days. Red and white cabbage will last longer – about five to six days.

Celery This should be crisp when bought and keeps best when bought unwashed. Store in a cool place or the salad drawer of a refrigerator. If limp, stand in cold water with a lump of coal.

Courgettes The skins should be firm and smooth. Store in a cool place or in the salad drawer of a refrigerator. Use within three or four days.

Cucumber Avoid wrinkly, yellowing cucumbers. Wrap in newspaper and store in a cool place or the salad drawer of a refrigerator. Cucumber stored in the fridge will perish more quickly when exposed to higher temperatures.

Greens (Spinach, Lettuce) Foliage should be green and healthy-looking. Discoloured leaves should be discarded immediately. Refrigerate in polythene bags after washing, to avoid moisture loss.

Leeks Avoid those that are discoloured or showing signs of wilting. Keep in the salad drawer of a refrigerator or in a cool place for four to five days.

Marrows The skin should be smooth and unblemished. When ripe, a thumbnail should pierce the skin easily. Store in a cool place for five to six days.

Mushrooms Avoid mushrooms that are wrinkling. As these dehydrate quickly, store in a covered container or a polythene bag in the refrigerator. Use within two to three days.

Onions Avoid bruised or sprouting ones. Keep in a dark, dry, cool place and use within a week.

Peppers (Red and Green) The skins should be firm and unwrinkled. Peppers will keep for a week in the salad drawer of a refrigerator, but wrap cut ones in foil first.

Potatoes These bruise easily, so handle with care and keep in cool, dry atmosphere covered with paper. Store in paper bags, not polythene and do not store near strong-smelling food.

Radishes Avoid radishes that have started to wrinkle. They will keep crisp for several days in the salad drawer of a refrigerator.

Roots (Parsnips, Carrots, Turnips and Swedes) These should be free from mud and with no worm-holes. Carrots and parsnips should snap cleanly. Store in a cool, dry well-ventilated rack. Do not store in polythene bags.

Sweetcorn The corn should be yellow and unwrinkled, with the leaves tightly wrapped around. Store in the salad drawer of a refrigerator and eat as soon as possible.

Tomatoes Choose firm tomatoes and store in the salad drawer of a refrigerator. If at all soft, use straight away, as chilling will make them softer. If the tomatoes are green and hard, they will ripen in a few days in a sunny place.

Watercress Choose fresh green leaves. When storing, remove diseased or discoloured leaves and place in a perforated polythene bag in the salad drawer of a refrigerator.

Points to Remember Wash thoroughly under running water, where necessary. Only peel skins when absolutely necessary, as most of the nutritional content lies just under the skin. Salt destroys vitamins during cooking, so add later. Only use enough water to half cover the vegetables and cook only until they are just tender. Never add bicarbonate of soda, as this destroys Vitamin C.

But most important of all: never throw away the water in which you have boiled the vegetables. Use as stock for soups, stews, drinks, casseroles, etc. This vegetable water is full of goodness, and pouring it down the sink should be constituted a crime!

WHAT'S IN SEASON?

This seasonal calendar of fresh vegetables shows what an incredible variety of vegetables is available all the year round.

★ Denotes the beginning of the main season.

January *Home grown:* beetroot, Brussels tops, Brussels sprouts, cabbages, carrots, cauliflower, celeriac, celery, curly kale, greens, Jerusalem artichokes, lettuce, mushrooms, onion, parsnips, potatoes, swedes, turnips and watercress.
Imported: artichokes★, aubergines, batavia, Brussels sprouts, peppers, new carrots, cauliflower, celery, chicory, Chinese leaves, courgettes, cucumbers, endive, fennel, lettuce, onions, potatoes, radish, salsify, sweet potatoes, tomatoes.
February *Home grown:* beetroot, Brussels tops, Brussels sprouts, cabbage, carrots, cauliflower, celery, curly kale, greens, Jerusalem artichokes, leeks, lettuce, onions, mushrooms, parsnips, potatoes, spring onions★, swede, turnips, watercress.
Imported: artichokes, aubergines, batavia, peppers, carrots, cauliflower, celery, chicory, Chinese leaves, cucumbers, lettuce, mange tout★, onions, potatoes, radishes, salsify and tomatoes.
March *Home grown:* beetroot, broccoli★, Brussels sprouts, cabbage, Cape broccoli★, carrots, cauliflower, greens, Jerusalem artichokes, leeks, lettuce, mushrooms, onions, parsnips, potatoes, spinach, spring onions, swedes, tomatoes★, turnips and watercress.
Imported: artichokes, aubergines, broccoli, cabbage, calabrese, peppers, cauliflower, celery, chicory, Chinese leaves, cour-

gettes, cucumbers, endive, fennel*, lettuce, onions, potatoes, radishes, salsify, spinach and tomatoes.

April *Home grown:* beetroot, broccoli, cabbage, Cape broccoli, carrots, cauliflower, cucumbers, greens, Jerusalem artichokes, leeks, lettuce, onions, mushrooms, parsnips, potatoes, radishes*, spinach, spring onions, tomatoes, turnips, watercress.

Imported: artichokes, aubergines, cabbage, calabrese, peppers, cauliflower, carrots, celery, chicory, Chinese leaves, courgettes, cucumbers, fennel, onions, potatoes, radish, salsify, tomatoes.

May *Home grown:* artichokes*, asparagus*, beetroot, cabbage, cauliflower, celery, greens, leeks, lettuce, mushrooms, potatoes, radishes, spinach, spring onions, tomatoes, watercress.

Imported: aubergines, beans*, peppers, carrots, celery, chicory, Chinese leaves, courgettes, cucumbers, onions, potatoes, sweetcorn*.

June *Home grown:* beetroot, broad beans*, cabbage, carrots*, cauliflower, cucumbers, lettuce, mushrooms, onions*, peas*, potatoes, radishes, spring onions, tomatoes, watercress.

Imported: aubergines, beans, peppers, carrots, Chinese leaves, courgettes, onions, potatoes, sweetcorn, tomatoes.

July *Home grown:* beetroot, cabbage, peppers*, carrots, cauliflower, celery, courgettes*, cucumbers, lettuce, marrows, mushrooms, onions, peas, potatoes, radishes, runner beans*, spring onions, sweetcorn*, tomatoes, watercress.

Imported: aubergines, beans, peppers, carrots, cucumbers, onions, potatoes, sweetcorn, tomatoes.

August *Home grown:* beetroot, cabbage, peppers, carrots, cauliflower, celery, courgettes, cucumber, leeks*, lettuce, marrows, mushrooms, onions, potatoes, radishes, runner beans, spinach, spring onions, sweetcorn, swedes*, tomatoes, watercress.

Imported: aubergines, cucumbers, onions.

September *Home grown:* aubergines*, beetroot, Brussels tops*, Brussels sprouts*, cabbage, calabrese*, peppers, carrots, cauliflower, celery, courgettes, cucumber, greens, leeks, lettuce, marrows, mushrooms, onions, parsnips*, pickling

205

onions, potatoes, pumpkins★, radishes, runner beans, spinach, spring onions, sweetcorn, tomatoes, watercress.
Imported: aubergines, cabbage★, peppers, cucumbers, onions, tomatoes.

October *Home grown:* beetroot, Brussels tops, Brussels sprouts, cabbage, calabrese, carrots, cauliflower, celery, Chinese leaves★, greens, leeks, mushrooms, onions, parsnips, pickling onions, potatoes, pumpkins, radishes, runner beans, spinach, spring onions, swedes, turnips★, watercress.
Imported: aubergines, cabbage, peppers, courgettes, cucumbers, onions, sweetcorn, tomatoes.

November *Home grown:* beetroot, Brussels tops, Brussels sprouts, cabbage, calabrese, carrots, cauliflower, celeriac★, celery, Chinese leaves, greens, Jerusalem artichokes★, leeks, lettuce, mushrooms, onions, parsnips, pickling onions, potatoes, spinach, swedes, turnips, watercress.
Imported: aubergines, cabbage, peppers, carrots, Chinese leaves★, courgettes, cucumbers, lettuce, onions, potatoes, radishes, tomatoes.

December *Home grown:* beetroot, Brussels tops, Brussels sprouts, cabbage, calabrese, carrots, cauliflower, celeriac, celery, greens, Jerusalem artichokes, leeks, lettuce, mushrooms, onions, parsnips, swedes, turnips, watercress.
Imported: aubergines, batavia★, cabbage, carrots, cauliflower, peppers, celery★, Chinese leaves, courgettes, cucumber, endive★, fennel★, lettuce, onions, potatoes, radish, salsify★, tomatoes.

VEGETABLES AND VITAMINS

Vitamin A Carrots, spinach, watercress and peppers are important sources of this vitamin. Also present in runner beans, Brussels sprouts, cabbage, lettuce, peas and tomatoes.
Vitamin B Group Potatoes, peas and beans.
Vitamin C Potatoes, Brussels sprouts, cabbage, cauliflower, peppers, spinach, greens, parsley, tomatoes and watercress.
Vitamins K and E Most green vegetables.
Iron Watercress and spinach are high in iron. Also present in peas and cabbage.
Calcium Cabbage, carrots, spinach, turnips and watercress.

Useful Addresses

Beauty Without Cruelty, 11 Lime Hill Road, Tunbridge Wells, Kent TN1 1LJ.

Compassion in World Farming, 20 Lavant Street, Petersfield, Hampshire.

The Fallen Angel, 65 Graham Street, London N1 8LA (the country's first vegetarian pub!).

Friends of the Earth, 377 City Road, London EC1V 1NA.

Greenpeace Ltd, 36 Graham Street, London N1 8LL.

Hunt Saboteurs, PO Box 19, London SE22.

League Against Cruel Sports, 83–7 Union Street, London SE1.

Lynx, PO Box 509, Dunmow, Essex CM6 1UH (an organisation set up to fight the fur trade and its attendant cruelties).

Organic Growers' Association, 86–88 Colston Street, Bristol BS1 5BB (sound advice on pesticide-free organic gardening).

Soil Association, Walnut Tree Manor, Haughley, Stowmarket, Suffolk.

Thompson & Morgan Limited, London Road, Ipswich, Suffolk.

Vegan Society, 47 Highlands Road, Leatherhead, Surrey.

Vegetarian Catering Campaign, 182 Mansfield Road, Nottingham NG1 3HU (a vegetarian catering service who will help you set up your own vegetarian co-operative in your home town. No fee charged!). Tel. 0602 585666.

Vegetarian Society (UK) Limited, Parkdale, Dunham Road, Altrincham, Cheshire, or at 53 Marloes Road, London W8 6LD.

Please enclose a large SAE with all enquiries.

Index

210

211

Arrow Health

☐ The Gradual Vegetarian	Lisa Tracy	£2.95
☐ The Food Scandal	Caroline Walker &	£3.95
	Geoffrey Cannon	
☐ The Alexander Principle	Wilfred Barlow	£2.95
☐ The Complete Book of Exercises	Diagram Group	£4.95
☐ Yoga for Women	Nancy Phelan &	£2.50
	Michael Volin	
☐ Health on Your Plate	Janet Pleshette	£2.50
☐ The Zinc Solution	Professor D. Bryce-Smith	£3.50
☐ Goodbye to Arthritis	Patricia Byrivers	£2.95
☐ Natural Pain Control	Dr Vernon Coleman	£3.50
☐ The Natural Dentist	Brian Halvorsen	£2.95
☐ Ageless Ageing: The Natural Way to Stay Young	Leslie Kenton	£2.95
☐ The Joy of Beauty	Leslie Kenton	£5.95
☐ Raw Energy	Leslie &	£2.95
	Susannah Kenton	
☐ A Gentle Way with Cancer	Brenda Kidman	£2.95
☐ Yoga for Backache	Nancy Phelan &	£2.95
	Michael Volin	

ARROW BOOKS, BOOKSERVICE BY POST, PO BOX 29, DOUGLAS, ISLE OF MAN, BRITISH ISLES

NAME ....

ADDRESS ....

....

....

Please enclose a cheque or postal order made out to Arrow Books Ltd. for the amount due and allow the following for postage and packing.

U.K. CUSTOMERS: Please allow 22p per book to a maximum of £3.00.

B.F.P.O. & EIRE: Please allow 22p per book to a maximum of £3.00.

OVERSEAS CUSTOMERS: Please allow 22p per book.

Whilst every effort is made to keep prices low it is sometimes necessary to increase cover prices at short notice. Arrow Books reserve the right to show new retail prices on covers which may differ from those previously advertised in the text or elsewhere.

Bestselling Non-Fiction

☐ The Alexander Principle	Wilfred Barlow	£2.95
☐ The Complete Book of Exercises	Diagram Group	£4.95
☐ Everything is Negotiable	Gavin Kennedy	£2.95
☐ Health on Your Plate	Janet Pleshette	£2.50
☐ The Cheiro Book of Fate and Fortune	Cheiro	£2.95
☐ The Handbook of Chinese Horoscopes	Theodora Lau	£2.50
☐ Hollywood Babylon	Kenneth Anger	£7.95
☐ Hollywood Babylon II	Kenneth Anger	£7.95
☐ The Domesday Heritage	Ed. Elizabeth Hallam	£3.95
☐ Historic Railway Disasters	O. S. Nock	£2.50
☐ Wildlife of the Domestic Cat	Roger Tabor	£4.50
☐ Elvis and Me	Priscilla Presley	£2.95
☐ Maria Callas	Arianna Stassinopoulos	£2.50
☐ The Brendan Voyage	Tim Severin	£3.50

ARROW BOOKS, BOOKSERVICE BY POST, PO BOX 29, DOUGLAS, ISLE
OF MAN, BRITISH ISLES

NAME ....

ADDRESS ....

....

....

Please enclose a cheque or postal order made out to Arrow Books Ltd. for the amount
due and allow the following for postage and packing.

U.K. CUSTOMERS: Please allow 22p per book to a maximum of £3.00.

B.F.P.O. & EIRE: Please allow 22p per book to a maximum of £3.00.

OVERSEAS CUSTOMERS: Please allow 22p per book.

Whilst every effort is made to keep prices low it is sometimes necessary to increase cover
prices at short notice. Arrow Books reserve the right to show new retail prices on covers
which may differ from those previously advertised in the text or elsewhere.

Bestselling Non-Fiction

☐ The Gradual Vegetarian	Lisa Tracy	£2.95
☐ The Food Scandal	Caroline Walker & Geoffrey Cannon	£3.95
☐ Harmony Rules	Gary Butt & Frena Bloomfield	£2.25
☐ Everything is Negotiable	Gavin Kennedy	£2.95
☐ Hollywood Babylon	Kevin Anger	£7.95
☐ Red Watch	Gordon Honeycombe	£2.75
☐ Wildlife of the Domestic Cat	Roger Tabor	£4.50
☐ The World of Placido Domingo	Daniel Snowman	£4.95
☐ The Sinbad Voyage	Tim Severin	£2.75
☐ The Hills is Lonely	Lillian Beckwith	£1.95
☐ English Country Cottage	R. J. Brown	£3.50
☐ Raw Energy	Leslie & Susannah Kenton	£2.95

ARROW BOOKS, BOOKSERVICE BY POST, PO BOX 29, DOUGLAS, ISLE OF MAN, BRITISH ISLES

NAME ....

ADDRESS ....

....

....

Please enclose a cheque or postal order made out to Arrow Books Ltd. for the amount due and allow the following for postage and packing.

U.K. CUSTOMERS: Please allow 22p per book to a maximum of £3.00.

B.F.P.O. & EIRE: Please allow 22p per book to a maximum of £3.00.

OVERSEAS CUSTOMERS: Please allow 22p per book.

Whilst every effort is made to keep prices low it is sometimes necessary to increase cover prices at short notice. Arrow Books reserve the right to show new retail prices on covers which may differ from those previously advertised in the text or elsewhere.

Bestselling Fiction

☐ Dancing Bear	Chaim Bermant	£2.95
☐ Hiroshima Joe	Martin Booth	£2.95
☐ 1985	Anthony Burgess	£1.95
☐ The Other Woman	Colette	£1.95
☐ The Manchurian Candidate	Richard Condon	£2.25
☐ Letter to a Child Never Born	Oriana Fallaci	£1.25
☐ Duncton Wood	William Horwood	£3.50
☐ Aztec	Gary Jennings	£3.95
☐ The Journeyer	Gary Jennings	£3.50
☐ The Executioner's Song	Norman Mailer	£3.50
☐ Strumpet City	James Plunkett	£3.50
☐ Admiral	Dudley Pope	£1.95
☐ The Second Lady	Irving Wallace	£2.50
☐ An Unkindness of Ravens	Ruth Rendell	£1.95
☐ The History Man	Malcolm Bradbury	£2.95

ARROW BOOKS, BOOKSERVICE BY POST, PO BOX 29, DOUGLAS, ISLE OF MAN, BRITISH ISLES

NAME ....

ADDRESS ....

....

....

Please enclose a cheque or postal order made out to Arrow Books Ltd. for the amount due and allow the following for postage and packing.

U.K. CUSTOMERS: Please allow 22p per book to a maximum of £3.00.

B.F.P.O. & EIRE: Please allow 22p per book to a maximum of £3.00.

OVERSEAS CUSTOMERS: Please allow 22p per book.

Whilst every effort is made to keep prices low it is sometimes necessary to increase cover prices at short notice. Arrow Books reserve the right to show new retail prices on covers which may differ from those previously advertised in the text or elsewhere.

Bestselling Fiction

☐ Toll for the Brave	Jack Higgins	£1.75
☐ Basikasingo	John Matthews	£2.95
☐ Where No Man Cries	Emma Blair	£1.95
☐ Saudi	Laurie Devine	£2.95
☐ The Clogger's Child	Marie Joseph	£2.50
☐ The Gooding Girl	Pamela Oldfield	£2.75
☐ The Running Years	Claire Rayner	£2.75
☐ Duncton Wood	William Horwood	£3.50
☐ Aztec	Gary Jennings	£3.95
☐ Enemy in Sight	Alexander Kent	£2.50
☐ Strumpet City	James Plunkett	£3.50
☐ The Volunteers	Douglas Reeman	£2.50
☐ The Second Lady	Irving Wallace	£2.50
☐ The Assassin	Evelyn Anthony	£2.50
☐ The Pride	Judith Saxton	£2.50

ARROW BOOKS, BOOKSERVICE BY POST, PO BOX 29, DOUGLAS, ISLE OF MAN, BRITISH ISLES

NAME ....

ADDRESS ....

....

....

Please enclose a cheque or postal order made out to Arrow Books Ltd. for the amount due and allow the following for postage and packing.

U.K. CUSTOMERS: Please allow 22p per book to a maximum of £3.00.

B.F.P.O. & EIRE: Please allow 22p per book to a maximum of £3.00.

OVERSEAS CUSTOMERS: Please allow 22p per book.

Whilst every effort is made to keep prices low it is sometimes necessary to increase cover prices at short notice. Arrow Books reserve the right to show new retail prices on covers which may differ from those previously advertised in the text or elsewhere.

A Selection of Arrow Bestsellers

☐ Voices on the Wind	Evelyn Anthony	£2.50
☐ Someone Else's Money	Michael M. Thomas	£2.50
☐ The Executioner's Song	Norman Mailer	£3.50
☐ The Alexander Principle	Wilfred Barlow	£2.95
☐ Everything is Negotiable	Gavin Kennedy	£2.95
☐ The New Girlfriend & other stories	Ruth Rendell	£1.95
☐ An Unkindness of Ravens	Ruth Rendell	£1.95
☐ Dead in the Morning	Margaret Yorke	£1.75
☐ The Domesday Heritage	Ed. Elizabeth Hallam	£3.95
☐ Elvis and Me	Priscilla Presley	£2.95
☐ The World of Placido Domingo	Daniel Snowman	£4.95
☐ Maria Callas	Arianna Stassinopoulos	£2.50
☐ The Brendan Voyage	Tim Severin	£3.50
☐ A Shine of Rainbows	Lillian Beckwith	£1.95
☐ Rates of Exchange	Malcolm Bradbury	£2.95
☐ Thy Tears Might Cease	Michael Farrell	£2.95
☐ Pudding and Pie (Nancy Mitford Omnibus)	Nancy Mitford	£3.95

ARROW BOOKS, BOOKSERVICE BY POST, PO BOX 29, DOUGLAS, ISLE OF MAN, BRITISH ISLES

NAME ....

ADDRESS ....

....

....

Please enclose a cheque or postal order made out to Arrow Books Ltd. for the amount due and allow the following for postage and packing.

U.K. CUSTOMERS: Please allow 22p per book to a maximum of £3.00.

B.F.P.O. & EIRE: Please allow 22p per book to a maximum of £3.00.

OVERSEAS CUSTOMERS: Please allow 22p per book.

Whilst every effort is made to keep prices low it is sometimes necessary to increase cover prices at short notice. Arrow Books reserve the right to show new retail prices on covers which may differ from those previously advertised in the text or elsewhere.

A Selection of Arrow Bestsellers

☐ A Long Way From Heaven	Sheelagh Kelly	£2.95
☐ 1985	Anthony Burgess	£1.95
☐ To Glory We Steer	Alexander Kent	£2.50
☐ The Last Raider	Douglas Reeman	£2.50
☐ Strike from the Sea	Douglas Reeman	£2.50
☐ Albatross	Evelyn Anthony	£2.50
☐ Return of the Howling	Gary Brandner	£1.95
☐ 2001: A Space Odyssey	Arthur C. Clarke	£1.95
☐ The Sea Shall Not Have Them	John Harris	£2.50
☐ A Rumour of War	Philip Caputo	£2.50
☐ Spitfire	Jeffrey Quill	£3.50
☐ Shake Hands Forever	Ruth Rendell	£1.95
☐ Hollywood Babylon	Kenneth Anger	£7.95
☐ The Rich	William Davis	£1.95
☐ Men in Love	Nancy Friday	£2.75
☐ George Thomas, Mr Speaker:	George Thomas	£2.95
The Memoirs of Viscount Tonypandy		
☐ The Jason Voyage	Tim Severin	£3.50

ARROW BOOKS, BOOKSERVICE BY POST, PO BOX 29, DOUGLAS, ISLE OF MAN, BRITISH ISLES

NAME ....

ADDRESS ....

....

....

Please enclose a cheque or postal order made out to Arrow Books Ltd. for the amount due and allow the following for postage and packing.

U.K. CUSTOMERS: Please allow 22p per book to a maximum of £3.00.

B.F.P.O. & EIRE: Please allow 22p per book to a maximum of £3.00.

OVERSEAS CUSTOMERS: Please allow 22p per book.

Whilst every effort is made to keep prices low it is sometimes necessary to increase cover prices at short notice. Arrow Books reserve the right to show new retail prices on covers which may differ from those previously advertised in the text or elsewhere.